The Organisation for Economic Co-operation and Development (OECD)

The Organisation for Economic Co-operation and Development (OECD) is one of the least written about and least understood of our major global institutions. This new book builds a well rounded understanding of this crucial, though often neglected, institution, with a range of clearly written chapters that:

- outline its origins and evolution, bringing its story fully up to date;
- present a clear framework for understanding the OECD;
- set the institution within the broader context of global governance;
- outline key criticisms and debates;
- evaluate its future prospects.

Given the immense challenges facing humanity at the start of the twenty-first century, the need for the OECD as a venue where the world's leading states can discuss, on an informal and ongoing basis, the conundrums of globalization has never been greater. The clarity and rigor of these chapters cut through the layers of misunderstanding and misconception that surround the OECD, often dismissed as a "rich man's club," a "think-tank" and "a consultative forum." This new book dismantles these labels to provide a holistic understanding of the organization.

This concise and accessible introduction is essential reading for all students of international relations, politics, and world history and affairs.

Richard Woodward is a Lecturer in political economy in the Department of Politics, University of Hull, U.K.

Routledge Global Institutions

Edited by Thomas G. Weiss

The CUNY Graduate Center, New York, USA

and Rorden Wilkinson

University of Manchester, UK

About the Series

The "Global Institutions Series" is designed to provide readers with comprehensive, accessible, and informative guides to the history, structure, and activities of key international organizations. Every volume stands on its own as a thorough and insightful treatment of a particular topic, but the series as a whole contributes to a coherent and complementary portrait of the phenomenon of global institutions at the dawn of the millennium.

Books are written by recognized experts, conform to a similar structure, and cover a range of themes and debates common to the series. These areas of shared concern include the general purpose and rationale for organizations, developments over time, membership, structure, decision-making procedures, and key functions. Moreover, current debates are placed in historical perspective alongside informed analysis and critique. Each book also contains an annotated bibliography and guide to electronic information as well as any annexes appropriate to the subject matter at hand.

The volumes currently published include:

35 The Organisation for Economic Co-operation and Development (2009)
by Richard Woodward (University of Hull)

34 Transnational Organized Crime (2009)
by Frank G. Madsen (University of Cambridge)

33 The United Nations and Human Rights (2009)
A guide for a new era, 2nd edition
by Julie A. Mertus (American University)

32 The International Organization for Standardization and the Global Economy (2009)
Setting standards
by Craig N. Murphy (Wellesley College) and JoAnne Yates (Massachusetts Institute of Technology)

8 **The World Intellectual Property Organization (2006)**
Resurgence and the development agenda
by Chris May (University of the West of England)

7 **The UN Security Council (2006)**
Practice and promise
by Edward C. Luck (Columbia University)

6 **Global Environmental Institutions (2006)**
by Elizabeth R. DeSombre (Wellesley College)

5 **Internal Displacement (2006)**
Conceptualization and its consequences
*by Thomas G. Weiss (The CUNY Graduate Center) and
David A. Korn*

4 **The UN General Assembly (2005)**
by M.J. Peterson (University of Massachusetts, Amherst)

3 **United Nations Global Conferences (2005)**
by Michael G. Schechter (Michigan State University)

2 **The UN Secretary-General and Secretariat (2005)**
by Leon Gordenker (Princeton University)

1 **The United Nations and Human Rights (2005)**
A guide for a new era
by Julie A. Mertus (American University)

Books currently under contract include:

Regional Security
The capacity of international organizations
by Rodrigo Tavares (United Nations University)

Global Institutions and the HIV/AIDS Epidemic
Responding to an international crisis
by Franklyn Lisk (University of Warwick)

African Economic Institutions
by Kwame Akonor (Seton Hall University)

Non-Governmental Organizations in Global Politics
by Peter Willetts (City University, London)

The International Labour Organization
by Steve Hughes (University of Newcastle) and Nigel Haworth (University of Auckland Business School)

The Regional Development Banks
Lending with a regional flavor
by Jonathan R. Strand (University of Nevada)

Multilateral Cooperation Against Terrorism
by Peter Romaniuk (John Jay College of Criminal Justice, CUNY)

Peacebuilding
From concept to commission
by Robert Jenkins (The CUNY Graduate Centre)

Governing Climate Change
by Peter Newell (University of East Anglia) and Harriet A. Bulkeley (Durham University)

Millennium Development Goals (MDGs)
For a people-centered development agenda?
by Sakiko Fukada-Parr (The New School)

Human Development
by Maggie Black

Human Security
by Don Hubert (University of Ottawa)

Global Poverty
by David Hulme (University of Manchester)

UNESCO
by J. P. Singh (Georgetown University)

UNICEF
by Richard Jolly (University of Sussex)

Organization of American States (OAS)
by Mônica Herz (Instituto de Relações Internacionais)

The UN Secretary-General and Secretariat, 2nd edition
by Leon Gordenker (Princeton University)

FIFA
by Alan Tomlinson (University of Brighton)

International Law, International Relations, and Global Governance
by Charlotte Ku (University of Illinois, College of Law)

Preventive Human Rights Strategies in a World of New Threats and Challenges
by Bertrand G. Ramcharan (Geneva Graduate Institute of International and Development Studies)

Humanitarianism Contested
by Michael Barnett (University of Minnesota) and Thomas G. Weiss (The CUNY Graduate Center)

Forum on China-Africa Cooperation (FOCAC)
by Ian Taylor (University of St. Andrews)

For further information regarding the series, please contact:

Craig Fowlie, Senior Publisher, Politics & International Studies
Taylor & Francis
2 Park Square, Milton Park, Abingdon
Oxford OX14 4RN, UK

+44 (0)207 842 2057 Tel
+44 (0)207 842 2302 Fax

Craig.Fowlie@tandf.co.uk
www.routledge.com

The Organisation for Economic Co-operation and Development (OECD)

Richard Woodward

Routledge
Taylor & Francis Group

LONDON AND NEW YORK

First published 2009
by Routledge
2 Park Square, Milton Park, Abingdon, Oxon OX14 4RN

Simultaneously published in the USA and Canada
by Routledge
270 Madison Avenue, New York, NY 10016

Routledge is an imprint of the Taylor & Francis Group, an informa business

© 2009 Richard Woodward

Typeset in Times New Roman by
Taylor & Francis Books

British Library Cataloguing in Publication Data
A catalogue record for this book is available from the British Library

Library of Congress Cataloging in Publication Data
Woodward, Richard.
The Organisation for Economic Co-operation and Development / Richard Woodward.
    p. cm. – (Global institutions)
Includes bibliographical references and index.
    1. Organisation for Economic Co-operation and Development. I. Title.
    HC241.W66 2009
    338.9–dc22
                2008054172

ISBN 13: 978-0-415-37197-1 (hbk)
ISBN 13: 978-0-415-37198-8 (pbk)
ISBN 13: 978-0-203-87577-3 (ebk)

Contents

Illustrations

Tables

Figures

Box

Foreword

The current volume is the thirty-fifth new title—several have already gone into second editions—in a dynamic series on "global institutions." The series strives (and, based on the volumes published to date, succeeds) to provide readers with definitive guides to the most visible aspects of what many of us know as "global governance." Remarkable as it may seem, there exist relatively few books that offer in-depth treatments of prominent global bodies, processes, and associated issues, much less an entire series of concise and complementary volumes. Those that do exist are either out of date, inaccessible to the non-specialist reader, or seek to develop a specialized understanding of particular aspects of an institution or process rather than offer an overall account of its functioning. Similarly, existing books have often been written in highly technical language or have been crafted "in-house" and are notoriously self-serving and narrow.

The advent of electronic media has undoubtedly helped research and teaching by making data and primary documents of international organizations more widely available, but it has also complicated matters. The growing reliance on the Internet and other electronic methods of finding information about key international organizations and processes has served, ironically, to limit the educational and analytical materials to which most readers have ready access—namely, books. Public relations documents, raw data, and loosely refereed web sites do not make for intelligent analysis. Official publications compete with a vast amount of electronically available information, much of which is suspect because of its ideological or self-promoting slant. Paradoxically, a growing range of purportedly independent web sites offering analyses of the activities of particular organizations has emerged, but one inadvertent consequence has been to frustrate access to basic, authoritative, readable, critical, and well-researched texts. The market for such has actually been reduced by the ready availability of varying quality electronic materials.

For those of us who teach, research, and practice in the area, such limited access to information has been particularly frustrating. We were delighted when Routledge saw the value of a series that bucks this trend and provides key reference points to the most significant global institutions and issues. They are betting that serious students and professionals will want serious analyses. We have assembled a first-rate line-up of authors to address that market. Our intention, then, is to provide one-stop shopping for all readers—students (both undergraduate and postgraduate), negotiators, diplomats, practitioners from nongovernmental and intergovernmental organizations, and interested parties alike—seeking information about the most prominent institutional aspects of global governance.

Organisation for Economic Co-operation and Development (OECD)

The OECD is an elusive institution. Although it figures prominently in the literature on global governance, few scholarly treatments of the institution exist. It has, as Richard Woodward puts it, "an ethereal character." The relative dearth of works on the OECD is problematic for a number of reasons. Not only is the OECD a major player in contemporary global governance, as a source of statistical data and a gathering point for ministers and technocrats from the leading industrial nations (and many of their principal developing country counterparts), the organization and the constellation of institutions of which it is part is intimately connected to the international system put in place at the end of the Second World War. Hence, it is also part of the Cold War politics and the "triumph of liberalism"[1] that followed the dismantling of the Berlin Wall. It is, and has been, a much under appreciated player in global governance, and the task of this book is to correct that oversight.

Like the World Trade Organization (WTO, the successor organization to the General Agreement on Tariffs and Trade, GATT),[2] the OECD's antecedents lie in a prior institution: the Organisation for European Economic Co-operation (OEEC). Again like the WTO, the OECD's predecessor institution was designed for particular and quite specific political purposes: to facilitate the reconstruction of Europe; to lock in place a market-based economic system; to enable US industry to benefit from the position of pre-eminence in which it found itself at the end of the Second World War; to stratify American power; and to act as a means of forestalling Soviet expansionism and communist ideology. These factors alone are compelling reasons for developing a better understanding of the OECD. The importance of the institution does not, however, end there. It has also played a key role in helping the advanced industrialized countries enhance their positions of economic pre-eminence in the post-war (and post-colonial) period; and it has been one of the primary institutionalized machineries by which the industrial states have given assistance to their developing counterparts, however problematically.

The OECD's development has not always been smooth. It has for years been perceived as an exclusive club for the world's rich nations, leading many to call for its dismantlement, especially during the periods when it acted as an effective secretariat for the North during the so-called North–South Dialogue.[3] Its very existence has been called into question on a number of occasions (with the end of the Cold War perhaps being the most significant). And its raison d'être has always owed more to the circumstances of its birth, and to the political climate of the time, than to a strict and coherent rationale. It is, in short, a curious institution.

Given the lack of scholarly engagement, finding a first-rate author to write a book for us on the OECD should have been a hard task. It would have been, had Richard Woodward not agreed to write it for this series. Richard has all of the qualities we seek in our authors—encyclopedic knowledge, an accessible and engaging writing style, and a commitment to quality. He is a first-rate author and we are proud to have him in our stable.

Richard lectures in politics and international relations at the University of Hull, UK. He specializes in international finance, the offshore economy, cities as financial centers, and the political economy of international crime, as well as in the OECD.[4] His work has attracted much attention and has been published in several leading journals. Richard's commitment to high-quality work continues in this volume. His account engages both the institution's past as well as its future.

We like to think that all of our books are required reading for anyone interested in global governance. Given the importance of the OECD as an institution and the relative dearth of good independent work on the institution, we believe that this is particularly true of this book. As always, we look forward to comments from first-time or veteran readers of the Global Institutions Series.

Thomas G. Weiss, The CUNY Graduate Center, New York, USA
Rorden Wilkinson, University of Manchester, UK
April 2009

Acknowledgements

Although I did not know it at the time, the genesis of this book dates to a paper on the OECD's harmful tax competition initiative delivered to a conference hosted by the Political Economy Research Centre at the University of Sheffield in 2002. As a callow doctoral student I had prepared my paper in good time and, so I thought, thoroughly investigated the most likely questions the audience was likely to ask. Initially things proceeded as planned. The paper seemed to have been well received and the questions broadly along the lines expected. However, any sense of smugness about my elaborate preparations dissipated when someone asked the innocent sounding question "What is the OECD?" I didn't honestly know. Nor, in the tortuous session that followed, do I recall making a particularly good fist of fielding the other questions from the floor: "How does the OECD work?"; "What does the OECD secretariat do?"; "Why is the OECD influential?"; "How do you become a member of the OECD?"; "How does the OECD relate to the other major international organizations?"

What did not occur to me at the time was to ask why a distinguished academic audience would be asking a Ph.D. student seemingly trivial questions about such a well known international organization. Nevertheless, vowing not to be caught out like this again I tried to find some answers. Quickly it became apparent that there was little substantive material on the OECD. I drew some solace from the knowledge that although I didn't know much about the OECD, no-one else seemed to either. Indeed, even the OECD's own publications were somewhat ambivalent about precisely what the organization did and how it contributed to global governance. This book, I hope, goes someway toward clarifying the OECD's role and answering the questions posed to me those many years ago.

In the writing of this book, there are a number of people to whom I am indebted. First, I would like to thank Rorden Wilkinson and

Thomas Weiss for conceiving, and inviting me to contribute to, the Global Institutions Series. The final product is much stronger for their thorough and perceptive feedback on earlier drafts of the manuscript, and they have shown boundless patience in the face of endless delays. My gratitude is also due to the many academic colleagues with whom I've discussed the OECD. I particularly wish to thank Andrew Baker, Peter Carroll, Ted Cohn, Anja Jakobi, Alexandra Kaasch, Bob Kurdle, Rianne Mahon, Kerstin Martens, Tony Porter, Steve McBride, Morten Ougaard, Tony Payne, Paul Sutton, Michael Webb, Russell Williams, and Robert Wolfe for their wisdom and insights. Likewise, I am grateful to the many OECD staff who have diligently answered my queries, in particular to Patrick Love whose enthusiasm for this project quickened its completion. I should also like to sympathize with Simon Lee, Justin Morris, and Colin Tyler, my friends and colleagues who have (for the most part with good humor) indulged my incessant diatribes about the importance of the OECD to world politics. My greatest debt, however, is to my parents, without whose continual love and support this volume could not have been completed.

Abbreviations

BIAC	Business and Industry Advisory Committee
BIS	Bank for International Settlements
CCNM	OECD Centre for Co-operation with Non-Members
CEEC	Committee of European Economic Cooperation
CERI	OECD Centre for Educational Research and Innovation
CFA	OECD Committee on Fiscal Affairs
CIIE	OECD Committee on Industry, Innovation and Entrepreneurship
CIME	OECD Committee on International Investment and Multinational Enterprises
CMIT	OECD Committee on Capital Movements and Invisible Transactions
CTPA	OECD Centre for Tax Policy and Administration
CSO	Civil Society Organizations
DAC	OECD Development Assistance Committee
DAFFA	OECD Directorate for Financial, Fiscal and Enterprise Affairs
DAF	OECD Directorate for Financial and Enterprise Affairs
DAG	OECD Development Assistance Group
DCD	OECD Development Co-operation Directorate
DEELSA	OECD Directorate for Education, Employment, Labour and Social Affairs
DNME	Dynamic Non-Member Economies
ECO	OECD Economics Department
EDRC	OECD Economic and Development Review Committee
EC	European Community
EEC	European Economic Community
EDU	OECD Directorate for Education
EFTA	European Free Trade Area

ELS	OECD Directorate for Employment, Labor and Social Affairs
EMEF	Emerging Market Economy Forum
EMS	European Monetary System
ENV	OECD Environment Directorate
EPC	OECD Economic Policy Committee
EPOC	OECD Environmental Policy Committee
EPU	European Payments Union
FATF	Financial Action Task Force
FSF	Financial Stability Forum
GATT	General Agreement on Tariffs and Trade
GNI	Gross National Income
G7	Group of Seven
G8	Group of Eight
G20	Group of Twenty
IAIS	International Association of Insurance Supervisors
ICCP	OECD Committee for Information, Computer and Communications Policy
ICT	Information and Communication Technology
IEA	International Energy Agency
ILO	International Labour Organization
IMF	International Monetary Fund
MAI	Multilateral Agreement on Investment
MCM	OECD Ministerial Council Meeting
MDG	Millennium Development Goals
NATO	North Atlantic Treaty Organization
NEA	Nuclear Energy Agency
NGO	Non-Governmental Organization
O-5	Outreach 5 of the G8
OAPEC	Organization of Arab Petroleum Exporting Countries
ODA	Official Development Assistance
OEEC	Organisation for European Economic Co-operation
OECD	Organisation for Economic Co-operation and Development
OPEC	Organization of the Petroleum Exporting Countries
OSCE	Organization for Security and Cooperation in Europe
PAC	OECD Public Affairs and Communications Directorate
PARIS21	Partnership in Statistics for Development in the 21st Century
PIAAC	Programme for the International Assessment of Adult Competencies

PISA	Programme for International Student Assessment
PSR	OECD "Pressure-State-Response" Model
PUMA	OECD Public Management Service
PWB	Programme of Work and Budget
QMV	Qualified Majority Voting
SEC	Special Economic Committee
SME	Small and Medium Size Enterprises
SNA	OECD System of National Accounts
STI	OECD Directorate for Science, Technology and Industry
SWF	Sovereign Wealth Funds
TAD	OECD Trade and Agriculture Directorate
TDS	OECD Territorial Development Service
TUAC	Trade Union Advisory Committee
UN	United Nations
UNCTAD	United Nations Conference on Trade and Development
UNDP	United Nations Development Programme
UNEP	United Nations Environment Programme
UNESCO	United Nations Educational, Scientific and Cultural Organization
UNFCCC	United Nations Framework Convention on Climate Change
WHO	World Health Organization
WP3	OECD Working Party Number 3 on Policies for the Promotion of Better International Payments Equilibrium
WTO	World Trade Organization

Introduction

On 30 September 1961 the Convention on the Organisation for Economic Co-operation and Development (OECD) came into operation and so was born "a unique forum where the governments of 30 market democracies [see Table I.1] work together to address the economic, social and governance challenges of globalization."[1] Despite rarely permeating the popular psyche the OECD and its predecessor, the Organisation for European Economic Cooperation (OEEC), feature in many defining moments of postwar economic history including the administration of the Marshall Plan (1948–51), the renovation of the European trade and payments system (1948–58), the resolution of the 1973 and 1979 oil crises, weakening resistance to the completion of the Uruguay Round trade negotiations (1986–94), the reconstruction of Eastern Europe following the collapse of communism (1990–2000), and the genesis of the Millennium Development Goals (MDGs). Moreover, the OEEC and OECD have provided a crucible in which some of the most important ideas, norms, rules, and principles underpinning contemporary global governance crystallized and, via interactions with non-members and a continuous cycle of surveillance and peer review, the vehicle through which they have been disseminated and upheld.

Unsurprisingly the OECD is routinely heralded as a leading organ of global governance, but sustained treatments of the organization's role and influence are sparse.[2] Most commentators resort to crude and sometimes misleading generalizations to describe the organization and its functions. For example, the OECD is habitually labeled a "rich man's" or "rich country's club."[3] Collectively its members do account for three-fifths of world Gross National Income (GNI)[4] but the accuracy of this depiction is belied by several wealthy countries including Israel, Singapore and Saudi Arabia lying beyond OECD membership, and widespread variations in economic and human development

2   Introduction

Table I.1 Members of the OECD–key indicators

Country	Date of OECD ratification	GNP per capita 1963 (US$ PPP)	GDP per capita 2007 (US$ PPP)	GDP per capita rank 2007	Human Development Index rank 2005
Canada	10 April 1961	2,263	35,729	11	4
United States	12 April 1961	3,090	45,790	4	12
United Kingdom	2 May 1961	1,564	35,134	16	16
Denmark	30 May 1961	1,700	36,223	10	14
Iceland	5 June 1961	1,440[1]	37,277	9	1
Norway	4 July 1961	1,537	53,701	2	2
Turkey	2 August 1961	230	12,216	48	84
Spain	3 August 1961	220[2]	30,587	22	13
Portugal	4 August 1961	304	21,497	31	29
France	7 August 1961	1,671	33,281	19	10
Ireland	17 August 1961	757	42,978	5	5
Belgium	13 September 1961	1,500	34,780	15	17
Greece	27 September 1961	464	33,274	20	24
Germany	27 September 1961	1,641[3]	33,450	18	22
Switzerland	28 September 1961	2,010	39,244	6	7
Sweden	28 September 1961	2,045	35,622	12	6
Austria	29 September 1961	1,076	38,106	8	15
Netherlands	13 November 1961	1,212	38,144	7	9
Luxembourg	7 December 1961	1,606	79,985	1	18
Italy	29 March 1962	899	29,981	23	20
Japan	28 April 1964	620	33,525	17	8
Finland	28 January 1969	–	35,124	13	11
Australia	7 June 1971	–	34,882	14	3
New Zealand	29 May 1973	–	26,110	26	19
Mexico	18 May 1994	–	12,780	47	52
Czech Republic	21 December 1995	–	22,982	29	32
Hungary	7 May 1996	–	18,912	34	36
Poland	22 November 1996	–	16,075	37	37
South Korea	12 December 1996	–	24,712	28	26
Slovak Republic	14 December 2000	–	20,188	33	42

Notes: [1] Figures for 1960.
[2] Figures for 1962.
[3] The 1963 figure is for the Federal Republic of Germany only.
Sources: OECD, "Ratification of the Convention on the OECD," available at www.oecd. org/document/58/0,2340,en_2649_201185_1889402_1_1_1_1,00.html (Accessed 13 April 2006); OECD, "The OECD Member Countries," *OECD Observer* no.13 (December 1964): 21–22; UNDP, *Human Development Report 2007/2008: Fighting Climate Change: Human Solidarity in a Divided World* (New York: UNDP, 2007), 230–32; World Bank, "Gross Domestic Product 2007, PPP," available at http://sitereso urces.worldbank.org/DATASTATISTICS/Resources/GDP_PPP.pdf (Accessed 1 September 2008); World Bank, "Population 2007," available at http://sitesources.worldb ank.org/DATASTATISTICS/Resources/POP.pdf (Accessed 1 September 2008).

amongst OECD countries (see Table I.1). In 1963, the per capita incomes of the poorest members were one-sixth of the OECD mean. As recently as 2007, the World Bank did not class a fifth of OECD members as "high-income economies,"[5] while Mexico and Turkey languish at 52nd and 84th positions respectively in the United Nations Development Programme's (UNDP's) Human Development Index.[6] When discussing its functions many commentators blissfully pigeon-hole the OECD as a "consultative forum," "think tank," or "a pool of statistical and economic expertise."[7] These epithets précis elements of the OECD's work but do not capture the true essence of the institution or reveal the significance of these activities for global governance. It is to this venture that this book is devoted.

The OECD Convention

Much of the confusion surrounding the organization's role stems from imprecision in the OECD Convention.[8] Article 1 of the OECD Convention states the aims of the organization shall be to promote policies designed:

(a) to achieve the highest sustainable economic growth and employment and a rising standard of living in Member countries, while maintaining financial stability, and thus to contribute to the development of the world economy;
(b) to contribute to sound economic expansion in Member as well as non-member countries in the process of economic development; and
(c) to contribute to the expansion of world trade on a multi-lateral, non-discriminatory basis in accordance with international obligations.

The convention envisaged the OECD prosecuting this mission by institutionalizing international cooperation between the organization's member states and, where appropriate, between member and non-member states. To this end, Article 3 commits signatories to:

(a) keep each other informed and furnish the Organisation with the information necessary for the accomplishment of its tasks;
(b) consult together on a continuing basis, carry out studies and participate in agreed projects; and
(c) co-operate closely and where appropriate take co-ordinated action.

The convention appears to bequeath the OECD a discrete set of objectives (promoting sustainable economic growth and development, maximizing employment and living standards, and nurturing the global trading regime) and unequivocal means to pursue them (cooperative endeavors between states). The reality is less straightforward. The convention is neither wholly prescriptive nor accords the OECD an exclusive or protected role in any policy domain. The convention highlights broad policy objectives but does not preclude the OECD colonizing new arenas in response to events or the foibles of members and other international organizations. Indeed the pursuit of blanket goals like promoting economic growth and maximizing living standards has necessitated the OECD's involvement with almost every facet of economic and social life, transforming it into a "restricted forum on virtually unrestricted topics."⁹ The convention's failure to ring-fence responsibilities for the OECD and its conferring roles in provinces where other agencies of governance are active leaves the OECD vulnerable to having its functions duplicated or sequestered and makes its impact difficult to isolate. This freedom to roam across a range of policy issues and its ambiguous relationship with other international organizations has resulted in an extraordinarily elastic body whose functional domain is in perpetual flux.

Likewise, the convention's insistence that the OECD will "promote policies" by nurturing collaborative ventures between member states assumes states are predisposed to cooperate. Theories of international relations disagree over many things but are united in their belief that cooperation in international affairs varies qualitatively and quantitatively and that there are legions of material and ideational barriers to international cooperation. The OECD is not immune to these pitiless truths of global politics. Hurdles to international cooperation do not miraculously melt under the heat of the OECD's deliberations. Power and sovereignty are ubiquitous considerations. The OECD is emphatically not a meeting of equals. The most powerful member states provide most of the funding, set the agenda, make or break agreements, and exert a vice-like grip over the membership and remit of key committees. In areas where states guard their sovereignty most jealously the OECD is either inactive, as is the case with defense and security, or sometimes runs aground, as it did over harmful tax competition (see Chapter 1). Moreover, unlike many other international organizations the convention does not invest the OECD with a system of formal rewards and sanctions that might induce cooperation or obedience to its ordinances.

The OECD and global governance: a framework for understanding

Global governance is "the sum of the many ways individuals and institutions, public and private, manage their common affairs."[10] Most commentators subscribe to the view that states, albeit in conjunction with a bevy of other actors, are the main repositories of political power and authority, and hence are the main "managers of common affairs." In the contemporary world, whereas the powers of the state cease at national borders, the scale of the common affairs they crave to manage frequently stretches across national borders and, in some cases, assumes planetary proportions. Managing these problems requires states to act in concert by enacting common rules to which they all adhere. Hence the literature on global governance lavishes considerable attention upon international organizations and other machinery liable to facilitate interstate cooperation; in fact, some equate it with little else.[11] The central contention of this book is that the OECD is a pivotal international organization because it sows the seeds of interstate consensus and cooperation that allow humankind to reap a greater capacity to manage our common affairs.

At first blush however, the prospects of the OECD sponsoring international cooperation look far from salubrious. Being devoid of the sticks and carrots available to other global institutions one mystery surrounds *how*, in a world where we cannot assume that the preferences and interests of participants initially coincide, the OECD achieves rapprochement. A second mystery is *why* actors would abide by cooperative agreements when there are no sanctions to discipline recalcitrant parties. Yet history is replete with examples where states have reconciled their differences through the OECD, and many believe the organization wields a "subtle discipline"[12] over national and global policymaking.

Before explaining how and why the OECD engenders international cooperation it is necessary to say more about the nature of international cooperation. For most people, notions of international cooperation conjure up pictures of world leaders convening at legendary meetings to sign ostentatious treaties to rid the world of war or pestilence or ward off ecological catastrophe. This image is probably one reason why some student readers of this book maybe inclined toward a career in international organization. Alas, seasoned international diplomats know that, for the most part, the realities of international cooperation are more mundane. The topics are monotonous and the processes and outcomes low key. Most of the topics discussed at the

OECD are of a highly technical nature, impenetrable to the layperson, some of which probably make little material difference to most citizens' everyday lives. Some may sneer at the OECD's abstruse international standards governing the official testing of agricultural and forestry tractors or those for labeling fresh fruit and vegetables, but they provide essential oil to the cogs of international commerce in those areas.

Most of the cooperative proceedings at the OECD are of the consultative and deliberative kind mentioned in the first two clauses of Article 3: namely gathering, exchanging and analyzing information, painstaking dialogue amongst technical experts from national governments and the OECD secretariat, the evolution of informal best practice guidelines to harmonize or render national policies of states mutually compatible, and surveillance of member policies. Periodically, these deliberations pave the way for more profound and overt outbreaks of cooperation contained in the latter part of Article 3, where states undertake coordinated action or agree to abide by prescribed rules. On the rare occasions where the OECD enshrines agreements in formal legal text, it normally takes the form of non-binding "soft law." It is this humdrum work for which the OECD is famed and which sometimes plays a germinal role in the spectacular agreements alluded to above.

The reason often given for the objects of our undertakings is "because it's there." The problem for those examining the OECD is, except to the discerning eye, it frequently isn't. With the ethereal character of its work, fluid remit, and a membership that "owes more to history than to logic,"[13] the OECD has "no widely agreed raison d'être, no clear purpose from which its functions could be derived, few very precise commitments which governments were pledged to carry out, and no simple goals which commanded public understanding."[14] In order to gain some analytical purchase on this slippery and amorphous institution and go beyond the simplified soubriquets normally ascribed to it, this book borrows from a number of analytical frameworks[15] to suggest there are four interrelated and overlapping dimensions to the OECD's role in global governance: cognitive (the incarnation of a community of countries sharing overarching values), normative (the realm of research, knowledge and ideas), legal (the production of international law) and palliative (a lubricant to the wider processes of global governance).

Cognitive governance refers to a less celebrated quality of international institutions, to be exact their role as the embodiment of the values the members hold sacrosanct and which stitch them together as a community. Despite some aberrations (periods of authoritarian rule in Spain, Portugal, Greece, and Turkey coincided with OECD membership) the OECD promotes itself as a troop of "likeminded"[16] countries committed to democratic and market oriented modes of governance. Originally this was ineluctably connected to the Cold War. The OECD personified a community of nations founded upon democratic and capitalist principles, vying for supremacy with authoritarian and centrally planned alternatives. The victory of these values in the Cold War served only to embolden the belief that the model embraced by the OECD and its members was one to which others should aspire. Today, the OECD symbolizes "the de facto standards for the ideal state in the contemporary world."[17]

The OECD countries' consensus on overarching principles is a promising start for international cooperation. Unlike more universalistic global institutions the OECD is not burdened by having to reconcile congenitally competing visions of global governance. Even liberal international relations theories, however, which proceed from the premise that states are inclined to cooperate because of broadly harmonious objectives (such as those in the OECD Convention) and preferences (such as an affinity for capitalism and democracy), accept that cooperation can be stymied by altercations over technical issues, clashing intellectual fashions, and mutual misunderstandings which cause participants to frame their interests in a contradictory manner. For example, in the nineteenth century, scientific disagreements about how diseases such as cholera and yellow fever spread postponed international cooperation for the best part of a century despite the common interests and objectives of states.[18] Normative governance refers to the "development and diffusion of shared knowledge structures—ideas"[19] at the OECD that make cooperative ventures more likely.

OECD activity revolves around a warren of committees and working groups populated by government officials, staff of the OECD secretariat, technical experts and sometimes civil society. By repeatedly bringing the same high-level policymakers together the OECD blends participants into "communities of influence"[20] that share perspectives on specific issues and the wider world, whose expertise shapes agendas in national capitals and international organizations. These communities are a "laboratory of policy concepts"[21] where experts from national governments and the OECD secretariat evolve common vocabularies vital to understanding and framing policy issues, statistics to enable comparison between economies, agreements about future courses of action, and benchmarks to assess national performances. Conventional wisdom on a host of issues such as "trade in services" or the principle that the "polluter pays" trace their origin to contemplations in the OECD.

Based on the experience of their peers, officials come away from OECD meetings with ideas about how to improve domestic policy-making. Moreover, as well as learning *from* each other, exchanges in OECD committees enable officials to learn *about* each other. Interactions inculcate government ministers and officials with a more nuanced appreciation of the dilemmas facing their counterparts abroad and "at minimum … the concerns of partners become a continuous factor in domestic policy-making."[22] Cyclic interactions in the OECD also generate expectations about standards of behavior amongst senior policymakers. Cognizance that they will shortly meet their peer group again at the OECD puts pressure on domestic officials to follow agreed undertakings to avoid loss of reputation. Normative governance is the vaguest dimension of the OECD but it is arguably through challenging and changing the mindsets of the people involved that the organization achieves its greatest influence.[23]

The OECD is primarily a forum for consultation, where states seek informal consensus on matters of mutual interest, rather than negotiation, where they seek formal rules or legal covenants to govern their behavior. Ironically, legal governance, the ability of states to conclude international agreements using the OECD's decision-making apparatus,[24] is probably the least important but most commemorated dimension of OECD governance. The organization's concords perforate almost every sphere of economic life, but it is not a prolific legislator. As of July 2008, there were just 231 legal acts in force (see Table 3.1), all of which take the form of "soft law" in the sense that although around one-seventh of OECD acts are legally binding, the commitments are imprecise and enforcement relies on surveillance and peer pressure rather than formal sanctions.

The confluence of cognitive, normative and legal governance gives rise to the final dimension which, for want of a better phrase, is termed palliative governance. Palliative governance is a portmanteau term encompassing the bundle of ways in which the OECD greases the wheels of global governance. The OECD plugs gaps in global governance by providing a sanctuary for issues that do not sit easily elsewhere and interrogating emergent or neglected areas of concern on behalf of the members. Few other international organizations match the breadth of the OECD's policy competence, making it especially adroit at dealing with problems entailing interdisciplinary research. The OECD also supplies "support services" to an assortment of other international institutions, especially the WTO and the Group of Eight (G8). This support is mainly of an analytical nature. By producing studies and reports, equipping them with reliable statistics and new diagnostic tools, the OECD can facilitate cooperative ventures elsewhere. As the chapter previously noted, ministers seldom return from an OECD meeting brandishing formally codified international treaties. However, the OECD is a venue where controversial themes can be prenegotiated, enabling OECD countries to take forward a corresponding caucus into formal negotiations elsewhere.

The book ahead

Given the immense challenges confronting humanity at the turn of the twenty-first century, the need for a venue where the world's leading states can discuss, on an informal and everlasting basis, the conundrums of globalization has never been greater. With an enviable record of soothing and resolving international tensions, unsurpassed analytical capacity stretching over every plausible domain of the global economy and many global institutions now emulating the "soft" governance mechanisms it pioneered, the OECD appears ideally placed to play this role. Nonetheless, changing geopolitical realities and stiffer competition from the "huge supply"[25] of prevailing governance mechanisms mean that, in its present form, the future of the OECD is not assured.

Chapter 1 examines how this has come about by charting the origins of the OECD, its evolution alongside the globalizing tendencies it and its members unleashed, and the role it has played in helping to manage economic flashpoints and undertaking the groundwork for major initiatives in partner global institutions. The roots of the OECD lie in the postwar European reconstruction process. In 1947, the United States famously offered Marshall Plan aid to repair war-torn European economies and quench the communist threat. What is sometimes forgotten is that the United States made the Marshall Plan conditional upon the recipient countries creating a permanent organization to decide how this financial support should be distributed. The resultant organization, the OEEC, did not prove a particularly effective utensil for dispersing aid. Nevertheless, it did prove popular as a place where national policymakers could convene regularly in an informal setting to discuss ways to manage their growing interdependence and learn from each other about policy preferences and experiences. Moreover, the members appreciated the transparency resulting from the OEEC's surveillance and peer review processes. Thus, at the end of the 1950s when the European economies had recovered, the Western countries, led by the United States, decided such a body should be retained but must be adjusted to recognize the changing balance of power in the transatlantic community and that interdependence was a global rather than a regional phenomenon. The creature that emerged from the OEEC chrysalis in 1961 had shed its European epidermis and acquired a development dimension to become the OECD. The chapter looks at how, over the next five decades, the OECD applied its expertise and soft law mechanisms to an ever-growing raft of policy problems, encompassed a growing and increasingly diverse membership, and solidified ties with non-members from around the globe.

Chapter 2 explores the OECD's organizational structure and decision-making procedures. Particular attention is paid to the tasks performed by the institution's core components, including the secretary-general, the council, the secretariat, the maze of committees and working groups, and how they work together to drive the OECD's work. This chapter also reveals how latitude in the OECD Convention has contributed to a considerable diversity of OECD bodies and growing input from non-members and civil society organizations (CSOs). While Chapter 2 focuses on *how* the OECD goes about its business, Chapter 3 considers *why* the OECD is able to convert this activity into influence in global governance. To do this the chapter fleshes out the four-dimensional framework described previously in this introduction. While noting the difficulties of measuring the OECD's influence, the chapter suggests that over a sustained period the organization's ideas have slowly seeped into national policymaking practices and have refined global governance in a number of areas. Chapter 4 evidences these claims by applying the framework to some of the contemporary issues vexing the OECD. This account does not seek to be exhaustive but by touring the subjects of sustainable economic growth, trade and agriculture, development, taxation, private sector governance, the environment, science and technology, energy, employment, education, and health the chapter gives the reader a feel for the range of the OECD's remit. Despite the organization's importance to these topics and its record of dulcifying economic crisis, the OECD has faced perennial questions about its place in global governance. Chapter 5 evaluates the program of reforms the OECD is undertaking to quash criticisms of its performance and secure its position in the anatomy of global governance. The chapter focuses on OECD's pending enlargement, its new ties with large non-member countries, engagement with CSOs, and its possible role as a permanent secretariat for the G8 system. Chapter 6 summarizes the OECD story and ponders the future of this eccentric and long-neglected institution.

1 Origin and evolution

This chapter charts the antecedence and origins of the OECD, its evolution, and the organization's triumphs and setbacks. In many respects, the OECD saga is about the organization and its members' ongoing attempts to acclimatize to a world of their own making. Contiguous with other multilateral economic institutions, the OECD and its precursor, the OEEC, have constituted key nodes through which leading states hunted rules to advance globalization and govern the consequences. Strikingly, the concerns at the crux of the OECD have barely altered. The itinerary cited in the 2006 Ministerial Council Meeting (MCM) communiqué including "ensuring economic stability and improving economic performance," "implementing economic reforms for growth and employment," and a "programme to strengthen and modernize the multilateral (trading) system"[1] is redolent of the founding convention and the first MCM communiqué of 1961. Similarly, the tools supporting the OECD's mission have throughout been peer review, surveillance and soft law.

The globalization of economic activity, however, engendered four subtle changes to the OECD's role and remit. First, the OECD went from an exclusively transatlantic club to boasting members from all but the African continent. Second, the OECD went from an organization that talked *about* non-members to one that talked *to* them.[2] The unfettering of economic activity coupled the fortunes of OECD members to non-member states, especially the emerging economic superpowers of the global South. Despite expansion, only five contemporary OECD members hail from outside the transatlantic zone, forcing the OECD to incorporate more fully into its work those non-members averse or unready to assume membership. Third, the OECD expanded functionally. Lowering barriers to economic activity entailed a welter of issues that members illuminated through the OECD and it steadily accrued responsibilities in areas as diverse as corporate governance, the environment, genetics, computer security and financial crime. In time, the OECD also moved from examining issues in isolation to considering how different domains interact and synchronize. The final change involved the genre of cooperative ventures pursued at the OECD. Lately, the OECD served less as a venue for countries to coordinate policies *internationally* and more as an institution where they strive to uncover appropriate *domestic* policies to meet their common objectives. The remainder of the chapter is partitioned into seven sections. The following two sections consider the origins and record of the OEEC, and the factors compelling its evolution into the OECD. The chapter pays particular attention to the hegemonic influence of the United States in the conception and infant development of these institutions. Sections three through six depict the OECD's performance under its first four secretaries-general. This periodization is partly one of convenience, a means of dividing nearly 50 years of history into manageable chunks, but also reflects the OECD Convention, which gives the secretary-general some latitude to influence the organization's trajectory and status. The third section examines the early years of the OECD under Thorkil Kristensen (1961–69). Despite being hemmed in by other major international institutions the OECD made a sound debut in the core areas of finance, trade, and development. The fourth section reflects upon the reign of Emile van Lennep (1969–84) and the OECD's consolidation amidst the aftershocks of the economic earthquakes of the collapse of the Bretton Woods system of financial management in 1971 and the oil crisis in 1973. Although the OECD was a salve for the oil crises and negotiations to further liberalize trade, there were signs of disenchantment with the organization's role and performance from amongst the membership. The fifth section describes how the OECD was overtaken by events under the leadership of Jean-Claude Paye (1984–96). The OECD's contribution to the completion of the Uruguay Round trade talks and panache for structural issues were overshadowed by the fundamental redrawing of the international system signified by the collapse of the Berlin Wall. Those viewing the OECD as a Cold War combatant wondered what role the OECD could possibly play in the "new world order"[3] proclaimed by President George Bush, Snr. The sixth section deals with the attempts under Donald Johnston (1996–2006) to rescue the OECD from oblivion by reforming the institution. The seventh section acts a conclusion. It précis the main achievements of the OECD and briefly introduces the present secretary-general, Angel Gurria and some of the key challenges he faces if the reforms of the organization are to be completed successfully.

Precursor: The Organisation for European Economic Cooperation (OEEC) (1948–58)

The OECD story begins in the wake of the Second World War. The ruinous effects of military conflict left European economies on their knees. The aerial bombardment of cities annihilated the housing, infrastructure and industrial capacity of European economies. The surviving industrial units remained on a war footing and the heavy casualties sustained during the war had depleted the workforce. Worse, the fortunes spent prosecuting the war had effectively bankrupted the treasuries of the major European powers, inhibiting the postwar reconstruction effort. In stark contrast, the U.S. industrial base was unscathed and, as a by-product of servicing the needs of its allies, the U.S. economy boomed during the war. The least heavily mobilized of the major combatants, the U.S. labor force retained the skills required to retool the industrial sector and to service the consumer goods market. Accounting for half the world's industrial production, with surplus capital to invest, and the only country to possess atomic weaponry, the United States was the undisputed hegemon and had enormous power to shape the postwar order.

Anxious to avoid the mistakes made after the First World War and counterbalance the communist threat posed by the USSR, the administrations of Franklin Roosevelt and Harry Truman used this power to pursue, quite against the wishes of Congress and the American public, a more proactive foreign policy. Under their auspices, a rash of international institutions appeared to promote international cooperation and deter another military conflagration. Somewhat surprisingly, given the importance attached to European unity and prosperity by the United States, it did not envisage a specific institutional apparatus around which European countries could coalesce or which would supervise European recovery. Between 1945 and 1947, the United States spent $9 billion to aid European recovery. However, most of this money was of an ad hoc or bilateral nature. For the most part, European states were left to orchestrate their own reconstruction through funding from the International Monetary Fund (IMF) and World Bank.

By mid-1947 it was apparent that this approach was improvident and ineffective. Dwindling international liquidity had paralyzed intra-European trade, aggravating the scarcities of food, fuel, and raw materials resulting from the harsh winter of 1946 and drought-ridden summer of 1947. At this point, with several European economies on the brink of collapse, growing social unrest, and communist parties making strides in France and Italy, the United States intervened.

The Marshall Plan

In June 1947, Secretary of State George Marshall motioned the U.S.A.'s willingness to donate the financial aid needed to salvage Europe's ailing economies through the European Recovery Program, known colloquially as the Marshall Plan. These arrangements were conditional upon European states multilaterally devising and implementing their own blueprint for reconstruction. In addition to the short-term humanitarian issue of preventing widespread starvation, from the point of view of the hegemon the Marshall Plan served three interrelated purposes. First, the U.S. required export markets if it was to sustain its economic prosperity. European recovery was essential if these states were to become robust trading partners and, in the interim, Marshall Plan funds could be used to purchase goods made in the United States. Second, it was envisaged that by forcing European countries to cooperate in drafting and executing a recovery plan they would boost European integration and avoid the regression into petty nationalism that had blighted the interwar period. Finally, the Marshall Plan was one of the first expressions of the "containment" doctrine of George Kennan, then U. S. ambassador to the Soviet Union, which held that U.S. "policy toward the Soviet Union must be that of a long-term, patient but firm and vigilant containment of Russian expansive tendencies."[4] A peaceful and prosperous Europe was vital to stop the spread of communism.

The inalienable logic of the Marshall Plan was not sufficient for the U.S. Congress which, fearing a loss of control or that the money might be squandered, insisted the Europeans instigate a continuing organization to oversee it. Having vacillated over whether or not to join the program, the Soviet Union decided not to participate and denied its satellites a similar right, and in July 1947, 16 countries (Austria, Belgium, Denmark, France, Greece, Iceland, the Republic of Ireland, Italy, Luxembourg, the Netherlands, Norway, Portugal, Sweden, Switzerland, Turkey, and the United Kingdom) convened a Conference on European Economic Cooperation in Paris. The meeting established a Committee of European Economic Cooperation (CEEC) and a coterie of technical groups to sketch the recovery program presented to the U.S. government in September 1947. Following U.S. backing for these proposals, the CEEC pondered the development of a permanent organization to administrate the Marshall Plan. The committee plumped for an institution betrothing members to promote trade liberalization, production, financial stability, and full employment.[5] Attempts by the United States and France to imbue the organization with supranational authority were opposed by the United Kingdom, Sweden and

Switzerland, who coveted intergovernmental arrangements. The inter-governmental view prevailed and, in April 1948, the aforementioned 16 states (with the United States and Canada as observers and later associate members) plus the Commanders of the French, and joint British and American zones of Occupation in Germany (West Germany assumed membership in 1949) signed the Convention establishing the OEEC. Secretary-General Robert Marjolin, a distinguished French economist, headed the organization.[6]

OEEC performance

Chroniclers of the period are ambivalent about the OEEC's performance and contribution to Western Europe's economic renaissance. Detractors point to the OEEC's ineptitude in discharging its cardinal function, namely apportioning Marshall Plan aid. U.S. hopes that the process of disbursing aid would advance European integration were dashed as haggling over funds sharpened divisions between European countries. Allocating aid was such an ordeal for the OEEC that within three years it ceded responsibility to the Economic Cooperation Administration, a U.S. government agency.[7] Aficionados, meanwhile, posit that the OEEC achieved astounding levels of cooperation given the precariousness of the situation, and praise its role in repairing Europe's faltering trade and payments system. Between 1948 and 1956, intra-OEEC trade rose by 272 percent and was a key factor propelling European recovery.[8] This spectacular expansion of trade owed much to two OEEC inspired initiatives, the European Payments Union (EPU) and the Code of Liberalization of Trade, both ratified in 1950.[9]

At the outset, currency inconvertibility and the tendency of countries to hoard their meager foreign exchange reserves inhibited intra-OEEC trade. Each country sought to maximize the export of goods and services that were not essential to reconstruction and to extract payment in convertible currencies (dollars or gold) to purchase essential materials on world markets. Sadly, the OEEC countries' fervor for remuneration in convertible currencies was not matched by a predisposition to make similar payments themselves. Bilateral trade and payment agreements provided an interim solution but foundered because they prevented countries from using surpluses with one partner to offset deficits with third parties. In contrast, the EPU was a central clearing house. Each month the deficits and surpluses accumulated through bilateral trade were computed and communicated to the Bank for International Settlements (BIS) which offset them to leave each country with a single debt or claim against the EPU. The EPU enabled states to trade by obviating the need for swift bilateral payments. The Code of Liberalization of Trade complemented the overhaul of the payments system. Under the Code's patronage, the percentage of private intra-OEEC trade covered by quantitative restrictions fell from 44 percent in 1950 to 6 percent in 1961.[10] The boom in European trade lessened the need to import goods from the U.S., allowing OEEC countries to accumulate dollar reserves and consolidate their financial position to the extent that by 1958 all EPU members had restored currency convertibility.

Judging the OEEC solely by tangible commodities belittles its significance because it overlooks the organization's methodological and ideational legacy. The dilemmas encountered during the Marshall Plan forced the OEEC to adopt embryonic versions of working routines, such as peer review, that endure in the modern OECD's surveillance practices. Initial dispersals of Marshall Plan aid were not as generous as the OEEC had hoped. European pleas for more money fell on deaf ears, leaving the OEEC to cope with the shortfalls. The OEEC beckoned members to submit economic programs detailing their external funding requirements. The OEEC secretariat then prepared analyses of national programs before they were "exhaustively and critically examined, in the various committees of the organization, by representatives from all other member countries."[11] Peer scrutiny had positive secondary effects, assembling enormous quantities of information and educating officials about the problems and priorities facing their contemporaries abroad. Officials were inculcated with the "habit of cooperation,"[12] unthinkingly taking the interests of others into consideration when they returned to make policy in national capitals. Lastly, the OEEC was a concrete expression of a community predicated on capitalism and democracy.[13]

From OEEC to OECD (1958–61)

In 1955, Rene Sergent succeeded Marjolin as Secretary-General. Sergent, a senior French bureaucrat and Marjolin's erstwhile deputy, inherited an organization robbed of its earlier zest by virtue of its own success. The restoration of currency convertibility and the rejuvenation of the European economy vanquished the predicament prescribing the OEEC's conception. Although the U.S.A. was still the undisputed hegemon, relative U.S. decline, together with quarrels about European political integration, elicited a reappraisal of the transatlantic settlement and the OEEC's metamorphosis into the OECD.

Powerful arguments lingered for conserving institutionalized transatlantic economic cooperation but the United States, in particular, felt the OEEC unbefitting for the task. First, the degree of cooperation realized under the OEEC's stewardship buoyed the transatlantic community. With OEEC committees encompassing energy, agriculture, industry, transport, labor, and tourism, the scope of economic cooperation looked potentially boundless.[14] Furthermore, an institutional apparatus was vital to handle the transatlantic interdependence fomented at the OEEC. The trouble was that changing economic circumstances violated the donor–recipient model upon which the OEEC was premised. Originally, the United States supplied aid and tolerated trade discrimination against their products because the political remuneration from European rebuilding and integration exceeded the economic cost. By the late 1950s, Western Europe's recuperation and the tribulations afflicting the American economy precipitated a recalculation of this position. The United States argued for a new organization where Western European and North American states could meet on an equal footing and which would distribute the burdens of economic adjustment more fairly.[15]

Second, Cold War enmities had intensified and the specter of communism loomed. In 1953, the USSR detonated its first hydrogen bomb and four years later flaunted possession of intercontinental ballistic missile technology by launching the earth orbiting satellite, Sputnik. The promulgation of the Warsaw Pact (a communist military alliance) in 1955 and the brutal suppression of uprisings in Poland and Hungary in 1956 reiterated Soviet command over Central and Eastern Europe. Concurrently the Western military alliance, the North Atlantic Treaty Organization (NATO), was in disarray after U.S. intervention in the Suez crisis ruptured relationships with France and the United Kingdom. This milieu redoubled the real and symbolic value of the OEEC as a pillar of Western unity, democracy, and capitalist prowess. The Cold War battleground was also twisting from an East–West to a North–South axis as decolonization created new suitors for the rival superpowers in the developing world. The United States feared that if ideas and development assistance were not forthcoming from the West then newly independent states might embrace the communist model. As a body appertaining to European development and designed to receive rather than generate aid flows, the OEEC was poorly situated to assist the developing world, enervating its utility as a Cold War player.

Conflicts over European integration expedited moves toward a revised transatlantic organization.[16] The festering schism between intergovernmentalists and supranationalists within the OEEC erupted into open warfare in 1958 when six members (Belgium, France, West Germany, Italy, Luxembourg, and the Netherlands) established the

European Economic Community (EEC), a common market with a common external tariff. The EEC's detrimental effect on their trade and fantasy of political union alarmed sundry OEEC members, the United Kingdom especially. The United States and France blocked U.K. overtures for an OEEC free trade area, the former inferring that it would discriminate against its exports and erode its balance of payments position, the latter that it would weaken EEC solidarity.[17] Anglo-French frictions culminated in the acrimonious dissolution of the OEEC Council's December 1958 meeting. Unable to conciliate between two major players, the OEEC ceased to be an effective institution and the council never met again.

Formal progress on a fresh transatlantic partnership began in December 1959 with a summit meeting in Paris of the leaders of France, West Germany, the United Kingdom and the United States. Their communiqué argued for an unofficial convocation of OEEC members to consider how consultations on trade, development and regional economic integration should proceed thereafter. In January 1960, plenipotentiaries of 13 countries and the EEC met as the Special Economic Committee (SEC) and appointed the Group of Four on Economic Organization to consult with OEEC governments and the EEC about the institutional specifications of transatlantic economic cooperation. Their testimony, *A Remodeled Economic Organisation*, called for a genuinely transatlantic institution with Canada and the United States as full members and altering the nomenclature to the OECD to hint at concerns with economic development worldwide. A Conference on the Reconstitution of the OEEC approved the formula in May 1960 and commissioned a working party to devise a draft convention. Two months later a ministerial meeting endorsed the working party's labors and allotted a preparatory committee to finalize the convention and finesse the transition. On 14 December 1960, 20 states (the OEEC members (numbering 18 since Spain's accession in 1958)) plus Canada and the United States signed the convention and a supplementary protocol allowing the European Commission to participate in the OECD's work. The convention became operative on 30 September 1961.

Early years: Thorkil Kristensen (1961–69)

Life as the OECD began in solid, if unspectacular, fashion. The switch from the OEEC to OECD went largely unremarked and despite some internal reshuffling necessitated by the organization's transatlantic newcomers, the working culture was fundamentally unaltered and most policy sectors grandfathered into the new regime.

The inaugural MCM in November 1961 certified bold objectives for the organization's maiden decade, including a 50 percent expansion in real GNP amongst OECD members taken collectively, attaining price stability and equilibrium in members' external payments, reducing trade barriers, and fostering common approaches and cooperation in the field of development assistance. To begin with, it was unclear what the OECD would contribute to these tasks. For example, the restoration of currency convertibility and proclivity for global rather than regional trade liberalization drew discussion of financial stability and trade, two of the few policy arenas explicitly enshrined in the OECD Convention, into the ambit of the IMF and the General Agreement on Tariffs and Trade (GATT) respectively. Events conspired, however, to ensure the OECD's participation in the governance of international trade and finance and it "functioned steadily"[18] alongside these institutions to preserve a relatively benign international economic environment. The OECD also started to flex its pristine development muscles.

The first OECD secretary-general was Thorkil Kristensen. During two stretches as Denmark's minister of finance from 1945 to 1947 and 1950 to 1953 Kristensen was intimately involved in the execution of the Marshall Plan. Additionally his association with the Consultative Assembly of the Council of Europe (1949–58) familiarized him with the internecine wrangling that sullied the OEEC's twilight years. In short, Kristensen was well versed in the organization's ethos and the issues it countenanced, making him an ideal candidate to nurse the OECD through its childhood. Kristensen emphasized the normative dimension of OECD governance, maintaining that the "core of the OECD's work" was "the continuing process of *consultation* in the widest sense."[19] Incessant dialogue would "develop a common value system at the level of civil servants in the OECD countries that should form the basis for consensually shared definitions of problems and solutions in economic policy making."[20] The OECD secretariat was to accouter objective, scientific data and analysis to corroborate the process. For this reason, much of the OECD's primitive endeavor concentrated on technical questions such as ameliorating the speed, comparability and comprehensiveness of data and statistics, enhancing data dissemination, and perfecting the art of peer review.

International financial management

The organization's contribution to international monetary management in the 1960s verified the importance of these seemingly cosmetic changes and the strengths and boundaries of the OECD as a mechanism of governance. The Bretton Woods system of fixed exchange rates had brought a modicum of order to international monetary relations. From 1947 to 1960, the United States managed the system unilaterally, supplying liquidity by a constant outflow of dollars and stability by guaranteeing to convert dollars into gold at a fixed rate. The quandary was that the constant outflow of dollars ensured that foreign dollar holdings would eventually exceed U.S. gold reserves. This would destabilize confidence in the U.S. promise to exchange dollars into gold at a fixed rate, leaving the dollar vulnerable to speculative attack. A run on the dollar in November 1960 denoted the end of unilateral management and the genesis of a multilateral approach, albeit with the United States playing the lead role.

Largely dormant in the epoch of U.S. unilateral management, the IMF began to play a more assertive role in the late 1950s. Nevertheless, the rapidly expanding membership and European qualms about the power wielded in the institution by the United States undermined the IMF's desirability as a forum for superintending strains on the international monetary and financial system.[21] Decanting conversations to smaller institutions where European nations predominated, such as the BIS and the Economic Policy Committee (EPC) of the OECD, alleviated this. They too proved cumbersome and, at the behest of the Kennedy administration, the EPC crafted the more select Working Party Number 3 on Policies for the Promotion of Better International Payments Equilibrium (WP3). WP3 was composed of high-ranking officials from the central banks and finance ministries of Canada, France, Germany, Italy, Japan (after accession to the OECD in 1964), the Netherlands, Sweden, Switzerland, the United Kingdom, the United States, and delegates from the European Commission. Underpinned by the secretariat's surveillance, WP3 was a bi-monthly forum where systemically important economies could hold forthright and confidential exchanges about the impact of monetary and fiscal policies on the international financial system. Members anticipated that regularized interactions in WP3 could nurture progressive policy-making and peer pressure on states to prosecute strategies consistent with international payments equilibrium.

A famine of corresponding data upon which to base discussions diluted the efficacy of early WP3 meetings, as states could nullify scrutiny by rehearsing justifications of their approach based upon their own incontrovertible economic forecasts. The OECD's Department of Economics and Statistics adapted an IMF framework on uniform balance of payments statistics for use in WP3. Although far from flawless, this "common format for presenting the data, and bold, increasingly sophisticated projections of the trends by the OECD staff marked the transition to a franker discussion of national balance of payments adjustment policies."[22] Sentiments diverge about WP3's impact. Indubitably, WP3 meetings cultivated camaraderie and harmony amongst national officials about the workings of the international financial system. Their interactions presaged measures in other organizations such as the Group of 10's General Agreement to Borrow, and forestalled retaliatory deeds by creating informed divergence about national policies. Others, however, have professed it had a negligible impact on national policies and levels of international policy coordination in the 1960s. Even when deputies reached a strong consensus at WP3, they seldom educed decisive shifts in opinion in their own central bank or finance ministry, let alone the wider bureaucratic circles of national economic policymaking.[23]

Trade

Despite its salience to the convention the OECD appeared destined for a tangential role in the global trading regime. The OEEC's Code of Liberalization of Trade did not withstand the transition to the OECD. The widespread elimination of quantitative intra-European trade barriers in the 1950s meant the code was obsolete, but it was opposition from the United States and Canada which sealed its fate. Besides their aversion to an agreement they had not designed, the North Americans were apprehensive that European nations might deploy the code to perpetuate discrimination against their products. The North American countries also preferred a global approach to trade liberalization, championing GATT as the supreme institution for this enterprise.[24] Their optimism over GATT's capacity to conclude trade negotiations in isolation gradually evaporated and, by the end of the 1960s, its propensity for trade liberalization was often contingent on preliminary or parallel activity by the OECD.[25]

Under GATT, the central preoccupation was negotiating binding rules to reduce tariffs on industrial and manufactured goods, but in the 1960s controversial issues such as agricultural trade, trade related aspects of development, and non-tariff barriers appeared on its radar. These topics were less susceptible to GATT negotiations because states lacked consensual knowledge on which to base them. The size and heterogeneity of GATT's membership hindered the search for consensual knowledge. Whereas 26 countries participated in the 1960–61 Dillon Round trade negotiations, there were 62 in the 1964–67 Kennedy Round. The number of developing countries, whose agenda deviated from that of developed nations, swelled from seven in the Dillon Round to 25 in the Kennedy Round.[26] As frustration with the lethargic GATT escalated, the OECD Trade Committee, with ongoing meetings, smaller, more homogeneous membership and less legalistic approach, emerged as a prenegotiating forum to smooth the path of multilateral trade talks.

The case of government procurement exemplified the trade committee's role. States omitted government procurement from GATT's national treatment and most-favored nation principles, viewing it as a crucial component of national economic and security policy. With public expenditures consuming a rising proportion of GDP in OECD countries and the penchant of governments to indulge domestic bidders when awarding contracts, procurement rules were a noteworthy trade impediment. Major work at the OECD started in 1964 with the trade committee reviewing the procurement practices of members. Their report published two years later was the first wide-ranging comparative analysis of government procurement rules and revealed the extent of the bias toward indigenous suppliers. The OECD secretariat's draft text on government procurement guidelines appeared in 1967, followed by proposals from the U.S. and EC. By 1970, cogitation over these various proposals yielded a draft OECD code to liberalize government procurement. The code was non-binding but the substantive content, including the principle that rules should not prejudice against overseas suppliers, stipulations regarding exemptions, and mechanisms for monitoring compliance, became the fulcrum of government procurement negotiations in the 1973–79 Tokyo Round.

Development

OECD progress in development cooperation was mixed. The SEC installed the Development Assistance Group (DAG) in January 1960 as a forum for leading aid donors to talk about their philanthropic activities. Reconstituted as the Development Assistance Committee (DAC) following the transition to the OECD, it spearheads the organization's development exploits. The DAC does not dispense funds but is a location where the world's principal bilateral aid benefactors review, coordinate and evolve best practice guidelines in order to stretch the volume and effectiveness of official development assistance (ODA). The Development Centre, which became functional in 1964, buttressed the DAC's handiwork serving as "the OECD's strategic interface with the international development research community"[27] bringing insights to the organization about the idiosyncrasies of developing countries and transmitting OECD wisdom to the developing world. To this end, the Development Centre is a repository of knowledge, undertakes comparative research, arranges conferences and workshops, and solicits casual interchanges on themes unready for discussion in formal settings.

The impact of the DAC and the Development Centre mirrored that of the WP3 in that their effects were chiefly at a diagnostic or technical level and did not radically modify the contours of development assistance policy. The concept of bilateral development assistance was relatively new and DAC and Development Centre symposia permitted the exchange of experiences and information, a shared language to blossom, and confirmed a collective aid consciousness amongst directors of development programs in OECD countries.[28] This was not filtering through into more copious or effectual ODA, however, prompting the fifth high-level meeting of the DAC in 1965 to express "grave concern at the slow progress of development."[29] Peer evaluation of development policies through the Annual Aid Review may have spurred a slight softening of repayment conditions, but the DAC's first five years saw real ODA flows stagnate and the practice of aid tying (insisting aid is used to buy goods and services from the donor country) mushroom.[30] Toward the end of the decade, the DAC toiled to redistribute the burden of ODA. Nevertheless, for the majority of states, resource flows stayed substantially beneath the 0.7 percent of GNI ambition agreed at the United Nations General Assembly in 1970.

Consolidation: Emile van Lennep (1969–84)

Emile van Lennep became Secretary-General in October 1969 after eighteen years as Treasurer General of the Netherlands Ministry of Finance. Deeply immersed in global financial governance, van Lennep had held illustrious portfolios at the OECD including chair of WP3 and vice chair of the EPC and was a frequent participant in meetings of the IMF and World Bank. Under his leadership, the OECD consolidated its position, extending tentacles into Oceania through the accessions of Australia (1971) and New Zealand (1973) and newfangled issues. In 1970, the OECD was the first international organization to invent a dedicated Environment Directorate. By the time of van Lennep's farewell, 36 environmental instruments were in place covering, inter alia, movements of hazardous waste, water pollution, use and management, recycling, transfrontier pollution, prevention and control of oil spills, confining the impact of energy use, and a host of standards for collating, exchanging and standardizing scientific data.

The Directorate for Financial, Fiscal and Enterprise Affairs (DAFFA) and the Directorate for Science, Technology and Industry (STI) (the Directorate for Scientific Affairs until 1975) fathomed the challenges of international commerce. The DAFFA's best renowned ordinance is the 1976 Declaration on International Investment and Multinational Enterprises, setting voluntary benchmarks for corporate behavior and equal treatment of domestic and foreign-owned business. Thirty years later the amended Declaration perseveres as a leading manifestation of international norms to govern corporate behavior. Also enunciated through the DAFFA were templates to homogenize disclosure and regulatory requirements in international securities markets and cut tax avoidance, evasion and double taxation. The STI delved into the conundrums of saturated markets for steel and ships, consumer protection including prescient guidelines to safeguard personal data, and masterminded recommendations concerning cross-border cooperation between private insurance regulators.

Though microeconomic and "behind the border" matters leapt up the agenda in the 1970s, the promotion of compatible macroeconomic policies and cheerleading cooperative ventures in other forums were the nub of the OECD's role. Inevitably, the economic convulsions that punctuated the 1970s color assessments of the OECD's performance. The monetary instability, inflation, and lower rates of economic growth flowing from the breakdown of Bretton Woods in 1971 and the oil price hike in 1973, resonated throughout the decade, incubating material and ideational clashes amongst OECD members and between OECD and non-member countries. Exponents hold that the OECD's surreptitious steering of these tensions rescued the international economy from a reprise of the 1930s. Like his predecessor, van Lennep emphasized the normative element of OECD governance, declaring that "ninety-nine percent of our work concerns the exchange of experience and the elaboration of lines of action."[31] This unrelenting discourse reaffirmed the realities of interdependence and norms of international cooperation amongst OECD countries, abetting them to contain conflicts arising from inhospitable economic conditions and to make headway on a number of thorny issues surrounding trade and energy. Critics postulated the economic turbulence as evidence of the impotence of multilateral economic institutions to galvanize cooperation or, where cooperation occurred, to unearth prescriptions apposite to the new economic climate. This led to the refurbishment of living institutions and the flowering of others, such as the Group of Seven (G7), which diminished OECD prerogatives by trespassing on its core competencies.

Managing the oil crisis

In the fall of 1973, the oil producing cartels the Organization of Arab Petroleum Exporting Countries (OAPEC) and the Organization of the Petroleum Exporting Countries (OPEC) engineered a quadrupling of world oil prices by embargoing supplies to states siding with Israel over the Yom Kippur War. While OECD countries foraged frantically for funds to pay for more expensive oil imports, OECD envoys were machinating with OPEC leaders to recycle "petro-dollars" through the international financial system to provide liquidity to oil importers.[32] The public response was shepherded by the United States which, fretful about the West's energy supply and sensing an opportunity to heal wounds in the Western alliance caused by the Vietnam War, propounded a countervailing consortium of oil consumers.

As a body containing the world's prominent oil consumers, the OECD was a logical site to forge it and 16 countries adopted a Council Decision establishing the International Energy Agency (IEA) in November 1974. Lodged at the OECD and serviced by the secretariat, the IEA was an autonomous body with a separate governing board. This peculiar configuration reflected the fact that not all OECD members belonged to the IEA, most notably France, which interpreted the IEA as a contraption of U.S. hegemony. IEA members vowed to augment information about energy markets, magnify relationships with non-members, abate long-term oil dependency, maintain emergency oil inventories and, in the event of an oil supply disruption, institute a robust scheme of oil sharing and demand restraint.[33] Its clumsy response to the second oil-price spike of 1979 notwithstanding,[34] the credible concord between OECD oil importers has helped deter a recurrence of the scenario that gave rise to the IEA and its vigilance has smoothed the impact of actual and potential disruptions. The 1991 Gulf War, the Y2K Millennium Bug, the September 2001 terrorist attacks, and the damage resulting from hurricanes Rita and Katrina to oil production in the Gulf of Mexico in 2005 all saw IEA contingency plans invoked.[35] The IEA still bestrides the field of energy policy but changes with the priorities of members, and patterns of energy production and consumption altered the IEA's relationships and remit. The IEA now has 27 members (France eventually joined in 1994) and affiliations with over 100 non-member countries. The obsession with energy security persists but now envelops a variety of fuel sources, and energy efficiency and sustainability are palpable parts of the IEA schema.[36]

Trade

The deterioration in economic conditions provoked by the oil crises unleashed protectionist pressures imperiling trade liberalization. The less frenzied atmosphere and indefatigable schedule of the OECD checked this by chivvying along the Tokyo Round, sculpting the agenda for, and dowsing discord in, the Uruguay Round (1986–94), and clinching informal compacts on trade topics resistant to GATT resolution. One gambit was to eulogize about the felicities of trade liberalization and reinforce the pursuit as a norm common to OECD members. An ostensible example was the Trade Declaration at the 1974 MCM (and renewed every year until the completion of the Tokyo Round) subscribing members to avoid recourse to unilateral trade measures designed to augment their position at the expense of others. The Declaration was not enforceable and infringements and dispensations were commonplace, but contiguous with other OECD ministerial pronouncements, it was a momentous statement of what OECD members believed in.

After the disappointing outcome of the Tokyo Round, tentative steps toward a new GATT round began in the OECD. The 1981 MCM exhorted the secretary-general to trigger a program to examine immediate and longer-term trade issues and to produce a report by May 1982. The resulting project, *Trade Issues in the 1980s*, laid the foundation for the trade committee's input on agricultural and services trade without which the realization of the Uruguay Round would have been "inconceivable."[37] In both cases, the OECD induced change by bequeathing ideas and analysis that toppled entrenched mindsets. Until the 1970s, leading states did not deem services rightful ingredients of the GATT regime. Service transactions were not thought comparable to merchandise trade because while they regularly transcended national borders, they could not be transported or warehoused, and vendors often had to migrate with their product. Before services could be subject to GATT's disciplines the "idea" that services were tradable had to be established.[38]

The 1972 report of the OECD High Level Group on Trade and Related Problems first mooted the notion of "trade in services." The OECD's conscientiousness in fleshing out and popularizing the idea transformed attitudes and, a decade later, the bulk of OECD states were reconciled to services being legitimate targets of GATT rules. This did not mean services were ripe for GATT negotiation. Skepticism amongst OECD states about the purported benefits of liberalizing services trade and hostility from non-OECD members was one hurdle to prospective negotiations and another, reminiscent of government procurement, was "the absence of a theoretical foundation on which to construct a set of rules."[39] The OECD liquefied these obstacles by furnishing members with evidence about the importance of services to their economic wellbeing and developing "a conceptual framework for service trade modeled on fundamental GATT principles"[40] and services booked a place on the Uruguay Round negotiating agenda.

Unlike trade in services, agricultural trade was incorporated in GATT but immunities authorizing the use of quantitative restrictions and subsidies plus squabbles amongst major agricultural producers precluded negotiations. The OECD had extensively researched domestic agricultural issues, but not until the formation of a Joint Working Party of the Trade and Agriculture Committees in 1979 was there was any acute inspection of agricultural *trade*. Their 1982 report *Problems of Agriculture* demonstrated the profligacy and futility of domestic agricultural policies, their distorting effect on agricultural trade, and validated the idea that agriculture should be a topic for GATT negotiations. Under the rubric of the Ministerial Trade Mandate, the OECD turned to equipping negotiators with the knowledge and conceptual frameworks needed to consummate the talks. This included developing comparative aggregate measurements of domestic agricultural protectionism so that participants could pinpoint the likely impact of agricultural trade liberalization.[41]

The OECD continued to produce soft law instruments for trade topics proving intractable in the GATT. The most arresting achievement in the 1970s was in the field of export credits. Export credits are preferential terms offered by developed countries to encourage developing countries to purchase their products and facilitate their access to international markets. The onset of tougher economic conditions raised the specter of a race to the bottom, with developed countries gifting export credits to bolster the market shares of domestic producers. The OECD accommodated the quest for rules to govern export credits because all major export credit donors were members and, conversely, GATT contained net recipients of export credits who would oppose multilateral rules limiting it. Building upon previous research by the OECD's Group on Export Credits and Export Credit Guarantees, and assisted by the G7; 20 states approved the Arrangement on Guidelines for Officially Supported Export Credits in 1978. The arrangement stipulates the most charitable export credit terms that signatory states may offer.

The changing of the guard

Amidst this, the economic philosophy permeating OECD ideas and analysis was shifting. Van Lennep's tutelage proselytized the OECD from a loyal crusader for the Keynesian demand management gospel to an unashamed preacher of the supply side creed. The OECD secretariat syndicated reports censuring precepts of the Keynesian consensus and espousing supply side dogmas as early as 1970. It was not until the end of the decade, however, that the mantra of low inflation, monetary and fiscal discipline, and structural adaptation surfaced as a coherent package in country reviews, ministerial communiqués and landmark OECD studies such as the McCracken Report. What is less discernable is if the OECD was the "ideational artist" in the vanguard of this intellectual revolution or an "ideational agent," condoning already existing trends to ingratiate it with national capitals and international institutions.[42] The former viewpoint acclaims the OECD as progenitor and propagator of the new economic paradigm. As Keynesianism's elegant edifice crumbled, national elites seized upon OECD thinking to justify the enactment of supply side medicines.[43] Viewing the OECD purely as an ideational artist is problematic because of the miscellaneous messages emanating from the organization. OECD declarations indicated impetus for supply side doctrines nonetheless, the secretariat vehemently supported the U.S. Carter administration's "locomotive" strategy of macroeconomic reflation between 1976 and 1978 and was frozen out of G7 Summit preparations in the early 1980s having been denounced as "too Keynesian" by U.S. President Reagan and U.K. Prime Minister Margaret Thatcher.[44] Moreover, the OECD's supply side rhetoric only gains momentum once leading states, especially the United Kingdom and the United States, openly disputed and started to dismantle central tenets of the Keynesian consensus.

Van Lennep lobbied skillfully on the OECD's behalf but voices reproving the organization got louder as his reign progressed.[45] Institutions encroaching on the OECD's historical strongholds jeopardized its position. In development, the World Bank was providing "much of the necessary research, coordination, setting of standards, goals etc., that came mainly from the DAC a decade ago."[46] Likewise, the reform of the IMF's Articles of Agreement after Bretton Woods' demise shrank the OECD's economic surveillance duties.[47] The OECD's grip on macroeconomic policy coordination slackened after 1975 when leading members began making commitments in the G7 family. The G7 tried to coexist with the OECD, staging the summit at a moment where it could take MCM deliberations into account and, from 1977 to 1980, letting the EPC prime the macroeconomic portion of the summit agenda. This arrangement petered out when the outlook of G7 states digressed from that of the OECD secretariat.[48] To relieve the load on the crowded summit timetable, a posse of G7 ministerial groupings materialized. The Quadrilateral Group of Trade Ministers (the Quad) and the finance ministers and central bank governors impinged directly on the OECD's customary terrain. For example, the finance ministers discussed balance of payments imbalances and devised international efforts to manage them such as the Plaza Accord (1985) and Louvre Accord (1987), consigning WP3 to the sidelines.[49] Revitalized European integration was the foremost menace, however. In the beginning, the EEC's creation sapped the morale and quality of the OECD secretariat as talented personnel, lured by the relative lucidity of purpose and supranational vocation, departed for the European Commission.[50] The stuttering of the European project and burgeoning influence of the OECD staunched this flow, but between 1973 and 1986 European Community (EC) membership doubled, direct elections to the European Parliament were held, and hesitant steps toward monetary union were taken with the introduction of the European Monetary System (EMS). Those agitating to hasten European integration gained the ascendancy, paving the way for the Single European Act of 1986 which promised a single European market, reinforcement of EC bodies, and extensions to the organization's supranational endowments. Roused from its stupor, the EC was a serious regional competitor to the OECD. The EC comprised half the OECD's members and its proficiency on a breadth of issues made it an attractive venue for their cooperative expeditions.

Overtaken by events: Jean-Claude Paye (1984–96)

Jean-Claude Paye, a French bureaucrat and diplomat, was enthroned as OECD secretary-general in October 1984. Eminent postings in the European Commission and French government, latterly as the Director for Economic and Financial Affairs in the Ministry of External Relations, bestowed Paye a firm grasp of OECD politics. During his tenure, the newfound predilection for "structural" and supply side policies partially resurrected intrigue in the OECD. Having dissected them for a quarter of a century or more, the OECD had a comparative advantage in subjects like labor markets, taxation, competition policy, environmental sustainability, technology, education, health, and public sector governance that were suddenly in vogue. Furthermore, the span of the OECD's portfolio left it inimitably placed to diagnose relationships between these traditionally compartmentalized policy areas, so-called horizontal work. Regrettably, in an age characterized by harsher institutional competition and geopolitical upheavals, this did not assuage accusations pertaining to the OECD's relevance and its place in the anatomy of global governance looked increasingly untenable.[51]

Echoing his forebears, Paye stressed the normative dimension of OECD governance. He visualized the organization as an "analyst and catalyst"[52] imparting the raw materials (statistics, ideas, and recommendations) to promote policies beneficial to the world economy. The mutation of the OECD's recipe for success, however, and rumblings in elite opinion about the merits of policy coordination,[53] tweaked how the OECD would abide by the edicts of its convention. The OECD orthodoxy now supposed that to sustain non-inflationary growth, structural reforms that conquer obstacles to market forces and make economies more innovative, supple, and entrepreneurial must accompany the traditional manipulation and coordination of macroeconomic policy levers. Typical advice included introducing or extending competition by liberalizing product markets, slashing subsidies and privatization, making labor markets more flexible by promoting skills and encouraging the active participation of all social groups, and improving the quality of public governance and regulation. Thus, contrary to the 1960s and 1970s, the belief was that sustained non-inflationary growth rested not on *international* demand management but primarily on states pursuing the correct *domestic* policies, in other words "getting the fundamentals right." This had knock-on effects upon collaboration at the OECD, which was now less about attempts at formal coordinated action and more about identifying paramount domestic policies and deciphering a "'common policy culture' which ensures that approaches to policy in different countries reflect broadly common objectives and a shared understanding of the ways in which policies should be implemented."[54]

Structural policy

By the end of the 1980s, structural policy had achieved parity with macroeconomic policy coordination on the OECD agenda. Throughout the decade, time dedicated to structural issues by the EPC and the Economic and Development Review Committee (EDRC) expanded perceptibly as did the space devoted to them in their flagship publications, the *Economic Outlook* and the *Economic Surveys*. This did not satiate members' curiosity and, from 1988, successive MCM communiqués beseeched the secretary-general to beef-up analysis and surveillance of structural policies to mobilize peer pressure on members to eradicate structural rigidities. The apogee came in 1991 where over half the MCM communiqué was allocated to a litany of structural policy areas ministers wished the OECD to vet, including trade, agricultural reform, rural development, technology, competition policy, subsidies, shipbuilding, export credits, financial markets, foreign direct investment, labor markets, human resource development, social policy, migration, urban affairs, the environment, public sector management, and energy. This list was not exhaustive, with members at other times asking the OECD to apply its faculties to bribery and corruption, money laundering, cyberspace, and the implications of ageing societies. Disclosing the OECD's headway in all these fields warrants a chapter of its own, but key feats included:

- assimilating financial services into the Code of Liberalization of Capital Movements and the Code of Liberalization of Current Invisible Operations (1989);
- providing a base for the Financial Action Task Force (FATF), an intergovernmental body created by the G7 to develop policies to combat money laundering and later terrorist financing (1989);
- groundbreaking work to divine agreed environmental indicators, integrating environmental concerns into economic growth models, assessing the costs and benefits of climate change policies, analyzing linkages between trade and the environment, and launching a cycle of Environmental Performance Reviews to monitor countries' progress toward meeting their domestic objectives and international commitments (1993);
- broaching ideas, data and concepts to see the Uruguay Round to fruition (1993) and inquire into trade related aspects of domestic policies such as labor standards and industrial support;
- The *OECD Jobs Study* (1994) synthesized the secretariat's findings in labor adjustment, wage formation, trade, taxation, welfare, education, training, technology, and entrepreneurship to comprehend importunate unemployment in the OECD zone and stated nine broad policy guidelines to quell it. In 1995, the OECD affixed a tenth guideline and 70 detailed policy recommendations and the project became known as the OECD Jobs Strategy;
- a recommendation that states abolish tax deductibility of bribes for foreign public officials (1996) and begetting the Convention on Combating Bribery of Foreign Public Officials in International Business Transactions binding signatories to criminalize payments to civil servants overseas (1997);
- the gestation of guidelines for improving the quality of government regulation (1995), cryptography policy (1997), and changes to competition law to annul anti-competitive practices in international trade (1995).

Structural issues reanimated OECD–G7 relations.[55] The G7's forays into macroeconomic policy coordination met with modest success, but their high-level political meetings could not grapple with the technical complexities of structural issues. Communiqués released after G7 summit and ministerial gatherings exposed mounting reliance on the OECD. In the third summit cycle (1989–95), communiqués made 37 references to the OECD and its work compared with 26 during the first two summit cycles (1975–81, 1982–88) combined (see Table 5.5). The "G7–OECD nexus"[56] also changed qualitatively. References to the OECD in the first two cycles were reactive; all but one vindicated existing OECD work or pledged continued cooperation in the OECD. The G7 was more proactive in the third cycle, urging greater efforts from the OECD on seven occasions and asking it to investigate virgin territories on another six.

Reaching out to non-members

Perceiving the organization's fragility, Paye was unequivocal that the OECD should reach beyond its core clientele to service a hotchpotch of non-members. The Development Center had husbanded OECD non-member relationships, but now the organization began to engage more strategically with myriad non-members on a wider catalogue of issues. The Centre for Cooperation with European Economies in Transition (1989) and the Partners in Transition program (1991) conveyed OECD acumen to budding market democracies in Central and Eastern Europe. The Dynamic Non-Member Economies (DNMEs) initiative sanctified dialogue with emerging powers in Asia and Latin America, and many committees conjured working groups to survey developments in non-member states. In 1995, the DNMEs project morphed into the Emerging Market Economy Forum (EMEF), providing a more thematic approach to non-member involvement in the OECD. These kinships lubricated the accessions of Mexico (1994), the Czech Republic (1995), and Hungary (1996), and opened accession pathways for Poland, South Korea (both joining in late 1996), and the Slovak Republic (joining in 2000).

Unfortunately, the seismic geopolitical shifts incited by the cessation of the Cold War outweighed the recompense from the lionization of structural policies and the OECD's revised stance toward non-members. In 1989, the Berlin Wall that had sprung up a month ahead of the ratification of the OECD Convention tumbled. Amongst the rubble, according those who saw the organization as a Cold War warrior, lay the OECD's raison d'être. The disintegration of authoritarianism and central planning in Eastern Europe was a victory for OECD convictions about the superiority of capitalism and democracy as organizing principles for global governance, but bereft of plausible ideological adversaries the OECD looked anachronistic. The proposition that the OECD was NATO's economic limb was simplistic, but even the organization's sympathizers had misgivings about its suitability as a backdrop for fabricating the post-Cold War order. OECD members dominated global economic activity (see Table 1.1) but the "Big Six"[57] non-member economies (Brazil, Argentina, China, India, Indonesia, and the Russian Federation) were exerting a pervasive impression on an assortment of mysteries handled by the organization. Their exclusion made it arduous for the OECD to fully understand these issues, develop ideas, or conceive workable rules to govern them. DNME, EMEF and bespoke invitations to countries germane to specific sectors subdued these irritants, but non-members were not compelled by Article 3 to share information, consult continuously or cooperate where necessary or wholly subject to informal peer pressure arising from surveillance and peer review, blunting their effectiveness. Moreover, only a fifth of the planet's population resided in member states, prostrating the OECD's legitimacy as a fountainhead for global rules.

Table 1.1 Key global trends–OECD percentage shares

	1965	*1975*	*1985*	*1995*	*2005*
Population	20.0	18.5	16.8	17.4	18.0
GDP (nominal)	–	79.2	77.6	80.7	78.0
Merchandise trade imports	65.6	66.7	68.3	67.9	69.5
Merchandise trade exports	65.1	66.1	65.5	69.7	65.3
Forex	–	–	–	87.0	87.1[a]
Fuel CO_2 emissions	55.8	51.0	44.7	46.2	49.7
Bilateral aid	98.1	100	100	98.3	97.0

Note: [a] 2004 figure. All figures adjusted for OECD membership at the time.
Sources: Derived from the following sources: UN, *World Population Prospects: The 2006 Revision Population Database*, available at: http://esa.un.org/unpp/ (Accessed 20 June 2007); World Bank, *World Development Indicators Database*, available at http://siteresources.worldbank.org/DATASTATISTICS/ Resources/GDP.pdf (Accessed 20 June 2007). Carbon Dioxide Information Analysis Centre, *Online Trends: A Compendium of Data on Global Change*, available at http://cdiac.ornl.gov/ (Accessed 20 June 2007). OECD, *International Development Statistics Online*, available at www.oecd.org/dataoecd/50/ 17/5037721.htm (Accessed 20 June 2007). WTO, *Statistics Database*, available at http://stat.wto.org/Home/WSDBHome.aspx (Accessed 21 June 2007). BIS, *Triennial Central Bank Survey: Foreign Exchange and Derivatives Market Activity in 2004* (Basle, Switzerland: BIS, 2005), 12.

Reform: Donald Johnston (1996–2006)

In 1994, Paye's application for a third spell as secretary-general was rejected by a coalition of countries, marshaled by the United States and Japan. They branded his bureaucratic demeanor too languid to re-energize the OECD and backed the more politically heavyweight Canadian, Donald Johnston.[58] Johnston worked in the academic and legal professions before entering parliament in 1978. He went on to serve in Pierre Trudeau's cabinet (1980–84), most conspicuously as President of the Treasury Board. An ardent advocate of free trade, he rebelled against his party by voting for the U.S.–Canada Free Trade Agreement in 1988 and retired from parliament shortly afterward to resume his legal career. The snag was that the investiture of the Secretary-General requires unanimity and France steadfastly supported the incumbent's candidature. The standoff had not been broken by the expiration of Paye's term on 30 September 1994 and Staffan Sohlman, Sweden's ambassador to the OECD, assumed temporary charge until the anointment of a permanent successor. In November 1994, OECD members reluctantly accepted a compromise brokered by France and Canada extending Paye's tenancy until June 1996, after which Johnston would take the helm.[59]

At the 1996 MCM, members proffered their first non-European chief a modernization mandate. Their communiqué instructed the OECD to "accelerate the process of structural change. ... with a view to further enhancing the relevance, efficiency and effectiveness of the Organization."[60] Johnston underscored the normative dimension of OECD governance, describing it as a "'knowledge-based' organization committed to building expertise, intelligence, and advice for guiding policy action."[61] He deduced the OECD's flair for this was unencumbered because of the elasticity of the organization's remit, the quality of the secretariat, and an unrivalled capacity for interdisciplinary work. The deficiencies, he contended, were in the palliative dimension, namely the inability to circulate outputs in a timely, cost-effective manner or diffuse them to a truly global audience.[62] To tackle this the OECD embarked on a process of internal reorganization, outreach to non-members and civil society, and enlargement.

Modernizing the OECD

Banal though it sounds, internal revamping was inescapable if the OECD was to square the member's hankering for fiscal austerity (between 1996 and 1999 the OECD budget shrank by 18 percent in real terms)[63] with their thirst for pertinent diagnoses. The OECD effectuated the Executive Directorate in 1996 to oversee its assets and work program. It streamlined budgetary and management systems, purging outlays by a fifth and earmarking OECD resources to priorities nominated by members.[64] To emulate and interrogate the globalizing environment, the OECD rationalized directorates. Education, clustered for years with labor and social affairs, acquired an independent directorate in 2002 as members chased learning policies for the knowledge-based economy. DAFFA became the Directorate for Financial and Enterprise Affairs (DAF), losing responsibility for fiscal affairs to a new directorate, the Centre for Tax Policy and Administration (CTPA). The OECD clarified responsibility for research on public governance by amalgamating the Public Management Service (PUMA) and the Territorial Development Service (TDS) into the Public Governance and Territorial Development Directorate. To amplify influence in national capitals the OECD strove to speed decision-making and attract high-ranking participants to OECD committees.[65] Finally, in a gesture of fidelity, members indulged plans for a multimillion-euro upgrade to the organization's headquarters.

The second piece of the reform jigsaw was reaching out to non-members. Economic globalization trussed the affluence of OECD countries to that of non-member states, injecting urgency to the organization's pursuit of the Article 1 injunction to uphold principles, values, and policies to promote economic growth in non-member countries. Fortifying acquaintances with non-members was a chance to globalize OECD ideas and fight indictments over their legitimacy.

One element of the project was relations with non-member states and international organizations. The OECD spawned the Centre for Co-operation with Non-Members (CCNM) in 1998 to subsume the OECD's disparate liaisons with non-members and become the lynchpin of a sequenced, multilevel global relations strategy. Global Forums became the global level conduit for discussions with non-members. Forged in 2001, they are a hub for stakeholders from specific policy communities to tussle with themes transcending countries or regions especially "where the relevance of OECD work is dependent on inter-action and policy dialogue with non-members."[66] Today, 10 global forums straddle agriculture, competition, development, education, governance, international investment, knowledge economy, sustainable development, taxation, and trade. Regional and country-level initiatives embellished the global forums. Programs for Africa; Asia; Central and Eastern Europe, the Caucasus, and Central Asia; Latin America; the Middle East and North Africa; and Southeast Europe relayed OECD practices to these provinces and promoted dialogue on matters and actors unique to those regions. The final tier was the development of tailored linkages with individual non-members of cherished interest to the OECD. Schemes with Brazil, China, and the Russian Federation led the way. Dating back to 1992, the eldest structures are with the Russian Federation, since when it has undergone six *Economic Surveys*, dozens of peer reviews, joined various OECD instruments and now holds observer status in 83 OECD committees and working groups.[67]

The other dimension of the outreach program concerned civil society. Almost from the dawn, the OECD conjugated with organized labor and commerce through the Trade Union Advisory Committee (TUAC) and the Business and Industry Advisory Committee (BIAC) and OECD committees fixated with agriculture and the environment[68] routinely consulted CSOs. The OECD visits program, long-standing contacts with parliamentarians, information centers in Berlin, Washington, Mexico City, and Tokyo, and the bi-monthly *OECD Observer* provided additional avenues to speak with civil society. Nevertheless, a litany of civil society groups worried about the opacity of the OECD and admonished prominent directorates for staying aloof. The turning point arrived in 1998 when civil society outcry helped wreck the Multilateral Agreement on Investment (MAI).

The OECD's Codes of Liberalization have underpinned international efforts to liberalize capital flows.[69] Thus, the OECD seemed a sensible venue to undertake preparatory work pursuant to the negotiation of a binding multilateral framework of rules to liberalize and govern international investment. The Committee on International Investment and Multinational Enterprises (CIME) and the Committee on Capital Movements and Invisible Transactions (CMIT) wrestled with problem and the 1995 MCM enjoined them to finalize the MAI within two years. Negotiations were archetypically clandestine but in February 1997, Ralph Nader's Public Citizen posted a draft of the MAI treaty on the Internet. The document was condemned as an "investor's charter, privileging the pursuit of profit and eviscerating the ability of governments to pass legislation to protect consumers, workers and the environment."[70] Over 600 groups in 70 countries[71] battled to abort the MAI, outmaneuvering the OECD's consensus building efforts by rallying domestic political opinion against it. Fatally, the OECD granted endless concessions to keep the MAI afloat but this dampened the enthusiasm of those favoring the unadulterated agreement.[72] By the time the anti-MAI campaign climaxed in October 1998 with two days of direct action coinciding with an MAI negotiating session in Paris, domestic support had vanished and shortly thereafter the MAI talks were suspended.

The specter of further embarrassing casualties enfeebling the organization's standing in national capitals underlined Johnston's determination to enrich OECD–civil society relations. The showpiece reform, unveiled in 2000, was the Annual Forum. The Annual Forum unites emissaries from government, international organizations, business, and civil society to "share information, improve communication and foster a climate of enlightened policy making"[73] with the deliberations funneling into the subsequent MCM. Escorting the Annual Forum were renewed efforts to proliferate civil society admittance to Global Forums and OECD committees. The Civil Society Coordinators Network, containing at least one spokesperson from every directorate, pooled and circulated best practice about civil society engagement.[74] Civil society–OECD relationships oscillate across directorates but by the end of Johnston's term the OECD witnessed "a more heterogeneous set of civil society actors regularly assuming more substantial roles across a wider range of policy areas."[75]

Enlargement was the final tranche of the reforms. In December 2002, the OECD heads of delegation deputed a Working Group on the Enlargement Strategy to probe how enlargement would affect the personality and governance of the organization and delineate yardsticks for aspirant members. Their report, commended by the 2004 MCM, argued the organization ought to welcome "likeminded" and "significant"[76] states to contribute to the organization's work and heighten its global status, but warned this could accentuate financial shortfalls and produce a lackluster committee system. The OECD Council designated working parties and task forces to rework the organization's governance structures in expectation of a wave of accessions. The Council approved the resultant proposals in May 2006 (see Chapter 2).

OECD work

The mixed fortunes suffered by the OECD under Johnston illustrated why reform was pressing. The advent of the WTO and new trading powerhouses eclipsed the OECD's role in the multilateral trading system. The OECD has stalwart connections with the WTO secretariat and its prodigious research remains to prod multilateral negotiations. Nevertheless, the WTO impaired the Trade Committee's standing. As this chapter documents, officials used the OECD Trade Committee for candid discussion and prenegotiation between sporadic GATT meetings. Senior trade officials now grace the Committee sparingly because the WTO, as a permanent international organization, affords ample opportunities to meet in Geneva and many rows involve non-OECD members.[77]

Outside trade, the impasse confronting the harmful tax competition initiative confirmed the limits of the organization's authority and the veracity of the hazards posed by civil society. The harmful tax competition initiative targeted practices allowing wealthy citizens and corporations to shelter assets and avoid taxation in their country of residence. In 1998, all OECD countries except Switzerland and Luxembourg signed the Recommendation on Counteracting Harmful Tax Competition, obliging them to improve the transparency of their tax regimes and the exchange of information with foreign tax collectors within five years. Contentiously the OECD decreed 41 non-members must make equivalent commitments or face possible "countermeasures" from its members. Quite apart from the dubious legitimacy of its efforts to coerce non-members, the OECD was cryptic over the application of countermeasures to Switzerland and Luxembourg, abstainers from the recommendation and therefore not committed to extinguish harmful tax practices. Graver challenges arose in 2001 after the United States, petitioned vigorously by the tax planning industry and free market think tanks, withdrew support for elements integral to the harmful tax competition initiative. The OECD responded by ditching certain clauses and vouchsafing that the imposition of penalties on non-members would commence only after they applied to members. This second indulgence brought the project to a standstill because OECD countries cannot take action against non-members until they have quashed dissent within their own ranks, something that remains a distant dream.[78]

On the affirmative side of the ledger, the OECD's genius for interdisciplinary research married to its unrivaled policy repertoire soldered bonds with what was now the G8. References to the OECD in G8 communiqués jumped almost fivefold in the fourth cycle of meetings (1996–2002) and requests by the G8 for the OECD to initiate or intensify existing work trebled (see Table 5.5). The fourth and fifth cycles (2002–present) continued their fascination with structural issues and, flanked by requests from OECD members, gave impulses to OECD work on ageing societies, bribery, biotechnology and food safety, corporate governance and regulatory reform, development, e-commerce, education, environment, health, investment, and online security.

Faithful to the Convention, much of the OECD's work germinated from an interest in economic growth, especially the impact of information and communication technologies (ICT) and the "New Economy." In 1999, the MCM entreated the OECD to study the causes of divergent economic growth across OECD countries and spotlight ways to stimulate healthier long-term growth. The final report, *The New Economy Beyond the Hype* (2001), cautioned that ICTs were not a magic bullet. Harnessing the benefits of technological innovation and boosting productivity required macroeconomic prudence and structural reforms; points recapitulated in the 2003 publication *Sources of Economic Growth in OECD Countries.* Ideas for structural reforms poured from various directorates. The STI Directorate sponsored recommendations to protect consumers conducting electronic commerce (1999) and from cross-border fraud (2003), broadband development (2003), the licensing of genetic inventions (2005) and, in the aftermath of 9/11, recompiled guidelines on the security of information systems and networks (2002).

The OECD attuned its social policy work to economic growth by advocating policies to maximize the ability and willingness of individuals to engage in productive economic activity. Despite growing evidence that alternative approaches were as lucrative,[79] the EDRC pushed the broadly neo-liberal thrust of the Jobs Strategy (promoting an entrepreneurial climate, deregulating labor markets and wage setting institutions, and more miserly welfare systems). The then Directorate for Education, Employment, Labour and Social Affairs (DEELSA) was less captivated by neo-liberal ideas but nevertheless advanced "active labor market policies" to offset the phenomena of ageing societies and the shrinking numbers of people in work. DEELSA wanted changes to pension provision, early retirement, and improved training opportunities to entice older individuals to remain in the workforce. DEELSA also launched an investigation into how family-friendly policies could address low birth rates in OECD countries. Developing labor force skills constituted another flank of the Jobs Strategy. In 1997, in order to assist states to measure the performance of their education systems and formulate policies to foster lifelong learning, DEELSA launched the Programme for International Student Assessment (PISA). PISA measures the educational attainments of 15-year-olds on a triennial basis and is today amongst the most influential of the OECD's outputs.

The streams of work on economic growth complemented those on sustainable development and the environment. In 1998, environment ministers conscripted the OECD to formulate a new environmental strategy. Drawing upon the organization's nous in economic growth, agriculture, energy, science, technology, and social policy the strategy, endorsed by the 2001 MCM, identified 17 challenges and 71 actions for OECD states to secure sustainable development. To pressurize states to implement these policies the OECD stepped up surveillance of the environmental sphere, devising pristine indicators to measure progress and, from 2004, adding sections on sustainable development to all *Economic Surveys*. The OECD exercised its palliative function by lending expertise to the preparations and follow-up activities of a string of international conferences such as the 2002 World Summit on Sustainable Development. Additionally, since 1998, the OECD's Roundtable on Sustainable Development provides a location for ministers from member states (and non-member states from 2001) to meet privately with business and civil society groups for blunt discussions without undermining their publicly avowed negotiating positions.

Events, demographic change and the new millennium resuscitated established OECD work. The DAC boiled down the international community's multiplicity of development targets into six International Development Goals and suggested forging a worldwide development partnership to secure them. Unwittingly this kindled the process toward the MDGs flowing from the Millennium Declaration signed by 189 countries in 2000. Since the millennium, surveillance by DAC has sought to goad countries into meeting their pledges but, as Chapter 4 reveals, progress is limited. After the Asian financial crises of 1997–98, members called upon the OECD to elaborate corporate governance guidelines. In 1999, the OECD showcased its Principles of Corporate Governance, a set of shared non-binding standards sieved from the spectrum of corporate governance systems in member countries. The Principles, the first intergovernmental accord on corporate governance and revised in 2004 in the aftermath of the Enron debacle, are widely extolled as international best practice. The Principles are among the Financial Stability Forum's (FSF's) 12 Key Standards for Sound Financial Systems and guide the corporate governance element of the World Bank/IMF Reports on the Observance of Standards and Codes.

After entering into force in 1999, the Anti-Bribery Convention moved into the monitoring and compliance phase. By 2004, peer reviews of the legislative frameworks of all signatories were complete and showed them to be largely compliant with the convention. Elsewhere sections on core labor standards, the environment, consumer protection, and corruption found their way into the fifth revision of the Guidelines on Multinational Enterprises in 2000.

Finally, annoyance at the feeble showing of OECD health care systems in a survey published by World Health Organization (WHO) and the whim of the secretary-general breathed new life into the OECD's health dossier. Involving four directorates, the OECD Health Project ran from 2001 to 2004, measuring and explaining variations in the performance of health care systems in OECD countries and identifying instruments to help governments reconcile public health with spiraling costs stemming from demographic change and medical advances.

Conclusion: redemption? Angel Gurria (2006–?)

For nearly six decades the OEEC and OECD have worked furtively in the ongoing drama of global governance. If global governance had the equivalent of an Oscar ceremony neither organization would have won many, if indeed any, awards as a leading thespian. Nevertheless, they would have amassed a horde of gongs for "best supporting actor" for their performances in major productions such as the EPU, the oil crises, successive GATT negotiations, and G7/8 summit and ministerial meetings. Furthermore, the OEEC and OECD would have received countless honorable mentions in acceptance speeches for designing the stage on which the actors strut or the costumes they don. The OEEC and OECD have regularly established the modalities for formal negotiations or set frameworks of rules. The OECD is the leading, and in some cases the only, source of international rules governing a swathe of issues including export credits, taxation, pensions, foreign investment, multinational enterprises, corporate behavior, and a panoply of environmental matters. At other times the organizations stood in the wings to calm cantankerous artistes. By offering a private place where they could throw their tantrums, the OEEC and OECD built trust between sometimes warring actors and avoided public feuding likely to delay or destroy the overall production. Sometimes, as Chapter 3 covers in greater depth, the OECD detaches itself from the production to become the critic and review the performance of the central characters.

Nonetheless, when in December 2005 Johnston notified OECD ambassadors that he would not court reappointment, his heir knew that formidable challenges lay ahead if the organization was to reestablish its authority. Member states nominated six candidates for the post: Marek Belka (prime minister of Poland), Allan Fels (dean of the Australia and New Zealand School of Government), Seung-Soo Han (a former Korean politician), Alain Madelin (a French lawyer and parliamentarian), Sawako Takeuchi (a Japanese academic and government advisor), and Angel Gurria (former foreign affairs and finance and public credit minister of Mexico).[80] After the usual selection process (see Chapter 2) Angel Gurria, the first secretary-general hailing from a developing country, replaced Johnston in June 2006.

It would be premature to offer a full appraisal of Gurria's contribution to the OECD. However, a few preliminary observations are worth making. His vision of the OECD as a "knowledge bank"[81] evokes comparison with past secretaries-general about the normative dimension of OECD governance. Though Gurria is keen to salute the OECD's heritage, he is proving an energetic and entrepreneurial secretary-general, floating a flurry of initiatives to quicken the forward thinking, outward-oriented reforms fathered by Johnston. In 2007, the organization formed or reformed 32 committees and working groups, the most in any year of the OECD's history. These included a new OECD Health Committee and the reconfiguration of the Education Committee as the Education Policy Committee to direct the organization's health care and education mandates. The 2007 MCM also bore the secretary-general's inquisitive hallmarks. The communiqué launched two major projects, the OECD Innovation Strategy and the Political Economy of Reform. The Innovation Strategy will assess the contribution innovation makes to economic growth, productivity and development, and dwell upon its role in tackling emerging global challenges. The Political Economy of Reform program harvests information about country experiences with structural reforms and supports reform efforts by supplying policymakers with evidence and ideas to overcome vested interests. These themes plus a host of other contemporary issues being investigated at the OECD are picked up again in Chapter 4.

Gurria is also maintaining the reforming momentum at the OECD. The 2007 MCM resolved to launch accession discussions with Chile, Estonia, Israel, the Russian Federation, and Slovenia, and asked the secretary-general to "strengthen OECD cooperation with Brazil, China, India, Indonesia and South Africa through enhanced engagement programs with a view to possible membership."[82] Moreover, the G8 Summit in 2007 assigned the OECD as the platform for the G8's dialogue with the O-5 countries (China, India, Brazil, Mexico, and South Africa). Gurria's ruminations about consecrating the OECD's relationships with, or even becoming the secretariat to, the G8 and the Group of 20 (G20),[83] are unlikely to occur imminently, but the G8's decision perhaps marks a qualitative shift in the OECD–G8 relationship. Overall, Gurria has made a promising start. Whether he will accomplish the reform program and rehabilitate the OECD is a matter addressed in Chapter 5.

2 Organization and functioning

The previous chapter described the OECD's main achievements and failures. To advance the reader's understanding of how these issues arrived at the OECD and how they are then dealt with this chapter abseils into the bowels of the organization. Although a resolution on a new governance structure entered into force in June 2006, it made limited changes to decision-making procedures and did not fundamentally alter the roles and powers of the OECD's principal organs and offices.[1] Thus, the scheduled functions of OECD bodies still derive from the articles of the OECD Convention and the Rules of Procedure of the Organization, to which this chapter refers.[2] These documents allow OECD bodies leeway to institute their own working practices resulting in a spectrum of bodies and policy processes across the organization. The few universal rules include that all OECD bodies convene in private (Rule 5) at the organization's Paris headquarters (Rule 4b), and proceed in English or French, the two official languages of the organization (Rule 27) but even here the Council or Secretary-General may decree otherwise.

Starting with the member states, the chapter introduces the central protagonists in the OECD's work. Although many other bodies intrude on its deliberations, the OECD is a quintessentially intergovernmental organization whose members are at the reins. This is not to say that non-members plus individuals within the OECD cannot exert power, but to note that members govern the extent of their influence. The chapter then moves on to look at bodies responsible for the OECD's management and day-to-day work, namely the Council, the Secretary-General, the secretariat, and the labyrinth of committees and working groups. The Council is the OECD's executive chamber where members take collective decisions and direct the OECD work program. The secretariat supports the work program by acquiring and dissecting data, proposing policy ideas and providing administrative and logistical backing. The OECD committees and working groups are the place where government officials and selected civil society representatives gather with the secretariat to exchange information, contemplate proposals and review their implementation, including the conduct of the OECD's esteemed peer reviews. The final part of the chapter puts all these pieces of the OECD jigsaw together, showing how the interactions of these bodies drive the organization's work, and concludes with a detailed exposition of what is probably the best known and most revered OECD peer review process, the *Economic Survey*.

Who drives OECD work?

Member states

OECD members drive the organization, determining the substantive agenda and outputs in four ways. First, each member maintains a permanent delegation in Paris whose goal is to ensure OECD work reflects their government's priorities and to funnel OECD research back to national capitals. Primary responsibility for this lies with the heads of delegation who communicate the views of their government to other members and represent them in the council, the OECD's governing body. Other diplomats, notably the economic counselors, wield influence by serving on OECD committees. Second, OECD members supply most of the budget (Article 20.2), amounting to €342.9 billion in 2008. The OECD's core (Part I) budget accounts for around half of this funding and all members contribute according to the size of their economy (see Table 2.1). Supplementary (Part II) contributions

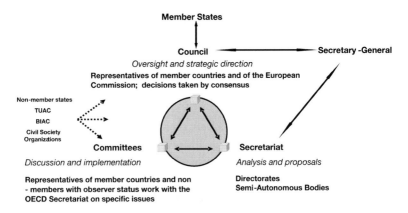

Figure 2.1 Who drives OECD work?
Source: adapteded from OECD, *Organisation for Ecomonic Cooperation and development*, available online at http://www.oecd.org/dataoecd/29/23/2397890.ppt (Accessed 7 August 2007).

account for another fifth of the budget and consist of money voted voluntarily by members and non-members to support particular work programs or the semi-autonomous bodies of the OECD such as the IEA (see Chapter 1). Not all members are necessarily involved and bespoke arrangements govern the participant's financial contributions. Salaries, pensions, and publications devour the surplus resources. Third, officials from member governments overwhelmingly dominate OECD committees, where the bulk of OECD work occurs. Finally, through the Council, members appoint the organization's executive-head.

Table 2.1 Scale of members' contributions to the OECD's core budget, 2008

Country	Contribution (%)
United States	24.98
Japan	16.01
Germany	9.14
United Kingdom	7.32
France	6.71
Italy	5.51
Canada	3.56
Spain	3.55
South Korea	2.42
Australia	2.14
Mexico	2.13
Netherlands	2.08
Switzerland	1.50
Belgium	1.40
Sweden	1.33
Norway	1.16
Austria	1.15
Denmark	0.97
Poland	0.96
Turkey	0.92
Greece	0.91
Finland	0.79
Portugal	0.70
Ireland	0.68
Czech Republic	0.51
New Zealand	0.44
Hungary	0.43
Slovak Republic	0.27
Luxembourg	0.22
Iceland	0.17

Source: OECD, "Scale of Members' Contributions to the OECD's Core Budget–2008," available at http://www.oecd.org/document/14/0,3343, en_2649_201185_31420750_1_1_1_1,00.html (Accessed 1 March 2008).

Notionally all OECD members are equal but in exactitude powerful members dominate. G7 countries donate almost three-quarters of the organization's Part I budget and can asphyxiate OECD programs by withholding funds. Furthermore, despite requiring Council approval, members can bankroll pet projects through Part II contributions. Similarly, 55 percent of OECD committee chairs and 52 percent of vice-chairs hail from the G7 (see Table 2.2) and only once has the chair of the lynchpin EPC strayed outside the United Kingdom, the United States, Germany, and Japan. Smaller countries also suffer because of a paucity of skilled personnel to staff their permanent delegations. Whereas larger countries sustain relatively bountiful missions to the OECD, smaller countries often post their most talented ambassadors to higher-profile international organizations.

One noteworthy anomaly is the "quasi-Membership"[3] of the European Union. Article 13 devolves representation of the European Communities to the Supplementary Protocol No.1 to the Convention, which states "the Commissions of the European Community. ... shall take part in the work of (the) Organization."[4] The European Commission is like an ordinary member in that it has a permanent delegation in Paris, a seat in the Council, may attend OECD meetings (Rule 7a), and engages in peer reviews and drafting OECD documents. Unlike ordinary members, the EU does not contribute to the OECD budget and is not entitled to vote when the Council is adopting legal acts.

Council

Under Article 7, the Council is composed of representatives from all member states and the European Commission and is the OECD's premier body "from which all acts of the Organization derive." The Council meets regularly at the permanent representative level when it is chaired by the Secretary-General (Article 10.2) and annually at ministerial level (the MCM) where a chair and two vice-chairs nominated by the Council preside (Article 8). Traditionally, the central participants at the MCM are ministers of finance, foreign affairs or trade accompanied by government officials, policy experts, BIAC, TUAC, and other OECD social partners, observers from multilateral economic organizations and, since 1999, observers from selected non-member countries. In 2008, the five enhanced engagement countries and prospective accession countries participated fully in the MCM for the first time.

Theoretically, the Council exercises corresponding functions and powers irrespective of the level of the meeting. It imparts strategic

Table 2.2 Chairs and vice-chairs of OECD committees (June 2008)

Country	Chairs	Vice-chairs	Total
United States	29	55	84
Japan	11	57	68
Canada	23	32	55
France	14	32	46
Germany	11	27	38
United Kingdom	19	15	34
Italy	10	21	31
Netherlands	10	16	26
Australia	10	15	25
Switzerland	9	14	23
Finland	1	19	20
Belgium	5	15	20
Mexico	6	12	18
Spain	2	16	18
Norway	7	9	16
South Korea	2	13	15
Austria	6	8	14
Hungary	2	12	14
Denmark	5	9	14
Sweden	5	7	12
New Zealand	3	7	10
European Commission	2	8	10
Greece	2	8	10
OECD	7	0	7
Czech Republic	1	4	5
Portugal	1	4	5
Ireland	1	3	4
Poland	1	3	4
Turkey	0	4	4
Luxembourg	2	1	3
Slovak Republic	0	2	2
Iceland	0	1	1
Non-member states	2	6	8
Others	3	6	9
Total	212	461	667

Source: OECD, "On-Line Guide to OECD Intergovernmental Activity," available at http://www2.oecd.org/oecdgroups/ (Accessed 30 June 2008).

control over the OECD by authorizing the Secretary-General to direct the secretariat to investigate certain subjects, scrutinizing their interim reports, adopting acts that bind members to varying degrees (Article 5, Rule 18), and making the final judgment about the accession of new members (Article 16). Council also provides administrative oversight by creating and shuffling ancillary bodies to enable the OECD to accomplish its aims (Article 9), and approving the budget (Article 20) and staff rules imposed by the Secretary-General (Article 11.1). In practice, however, meetings of permanent representatives tend to muse over routine matters whereas ministerial meetings are strategically oriented and lend the OECD political impetus. The MCM is the pinnacle of the OECD year, whose communiqué recapitulates OECD norms and outlines priorities for the year ahead. Cognizance that the MCM will adjudicate an issue can break deadlocks between officials and, where it does not, in-the-flesh talks between ministerial delegates at the MCM sometimes resolve the matter.[5]

Changes in the last two decades have compromised the Council's effectiveness. The ambassadorial merry-go-round and the saturation of the Council's agenda because of enlargement have diminished its ability to provide management oversight at permanent representative level. Likewise, the recent tendency of senior ministers from larger states to eschew the MCM weakens its mandate for shaping the organization's priorities. In the last five years, only two G7 finance ministers, Italy's Tommaso Padoa-Schioppa in 2007 and France's Christine Lagarde in 2008, attended an MCM, and appearances by G7 trade and foreign affairs ministers were scarcely more voluminous. The United Kingdom has not fielded any cabinet-level ministers since 2004, deputing senior economic officials instead.

To alleviate the burdens on the Council and afford it time to concentrate on strategic issues the 2006 resolution extended the devolution of operational issues to three standing committees operating under the Council's jurisdiction. The committees arrange business put before the Council, draft documentation in anticipation of council decisions, and advise on and verify the fulfillment of those decisions. Additionally the 2006 resolution overhauled the OECD's decision-making mechanism. The OECD takes decisions by consensus. Only in exceptional circumstances, and where members agree unanimously, do ballots occur on a "one member one vote" basis (Article 6.2). If a member feels it cannot support a resolution it abstains. In these instances, the resolution applies to all but the abstaining members. In July 2004, the OECD began experimenting with qualified majority voting (QMV). The 2006 resolution made these arrangements permanent, designating "special cases" where if a consensus cannot be attained a decision can be adopted providing it enjoys the support of 60 percent of members and is not opposed by three or more members who contribute a quarter of the Part I budget. Special cases include the approval or amendment of staff or financial regulations and rules, the formation, perpetuation or disestablishment of committees and programs, and, within limited parameters, the program of work and budget (PWB). Nevertheless, many strategic decisions including accession, participation of non-members, adoption of the overall PWB, revisions to the organization's governance structures, and the passage or amendment of OECD Acts still require unanimity.[6]

Secretary-General

As chair of the council (Article 10.2) and head of the secretariat, the Secretary-General is a critical valve linking national delegations with the OECD's everyday activities. All members can nominate candidates for the post of Secretary-General. OECD heads of delegation rigorously and extensively scrutinize the nominees through individual interviews and collective consultations. This process whittles down the field until a contender on which all OECD countries concur emerges. The council then appoints the individual as Secretary-General for a five-year period (Article 10.1).

The power of the Secretary-General is ultimately cramped by the need to retain the support of the membership and hence the council. Nevertheless, vagaries in the OECD governance structure give a politically shrewd Secretary-General the opportunity to leave their imprint. The Secretary-General determines the agenda of, and can make proposals to, any constituent body of the organization including the Council (Article 10, Rule 12). They decide how to discharge council proclamations and orchestrate the secretariat to that end. The Secretary-General keeps open the channels of communication amongst the multifarious OECD bodies and is the external face of the organization, brokering its wares in national capitals and international institutions (Rule 24). The secretary-general does not impinge blatantly on the trajectory of OECD committees but may occasionally try to manipulate the secretariat through their powers of patronage. Lastly, the Council appoints deputy secretaries-general on the Secretary-General's recommendation (Article 10.1). By convention, the OECD draws Deputy Secretaries-General from the different geographical wings of the organization. Four Deputy Secretaries-General, each supervising a discrete area or initiative, assist Angel Gurria (see Table 2.3).

Secretariat

The secretariat is the heartbeat of the OECD, exercising "all the functions necessary for the efficient administration of the Organization."[7] The secretariat subdivides into directorates and departments that

Table 2.3 Deputy secretaries-general of the OECD (July 2008)

Name	Nationality	Responsibilities
Aart Jan de Geus	Netherlands	• Political economy of reform • Preparing the MCM
Thelma Askey	United States	• Global relations
Pier Carlo Padoan	Italy	• Developing strategic vision • Relations with international organizations
Mari Amano	Japan	• Development • Policy coherence

parallel and service the Council and the Secretary-General, the OECD's semi-autonomous bodies, and OECD committees (see Figure 2.2). Recruited predominantly from member states, the secretariat is relatively large, numbering 2,488 in March 2008,[8] and exerts some independent power. Of particular salience is the cadre of approximately 700 professional economists, lawyers, and scientists within the secretariat who furnish OECD committees with administrative support, research, analysis, and proposals. This clan, consisting of high-flying bureaucrats seconded from national governments and renowned specialists recruited from the private sector, forms an impartial body that trades on its reputation and expertise to advocate and accustom committee members to innovative approaches to policy dilemmas.

The Secretary-General, the head of the secretariat, has permission to make recommendations to the council about what the secretariat should study, but the secretariat remains the servant of the members. David Henderson, former chief of the then Economics and Statistics Department, observes that while OECD commentaries "are prepared from an independent and transnational point of view, it is the clients— the member governments—that largely determine the choice, and *up to a point* the treatment, of the subject-matter."[9] States can ignore the advice and the secretariat's opinions gain less purchase where state interests are diametrically opposed. Importantly, however, the fact that states only choose the handling of the subject matter "up to a point" implies the secretariat has some wiggle room when determining how to execute a council edict. Moreover, because the OECD is frequently the first international organization to interrogate a policy issue systematically, the secretariat's analysis can have an enduring impact on its long-term bearing. By considering predicaments in revolutionary ways, the secretariat can highlight common ground or promote shared analysis of mutual problems that help to reshape national interests and enhance the prospects for future cooperation.

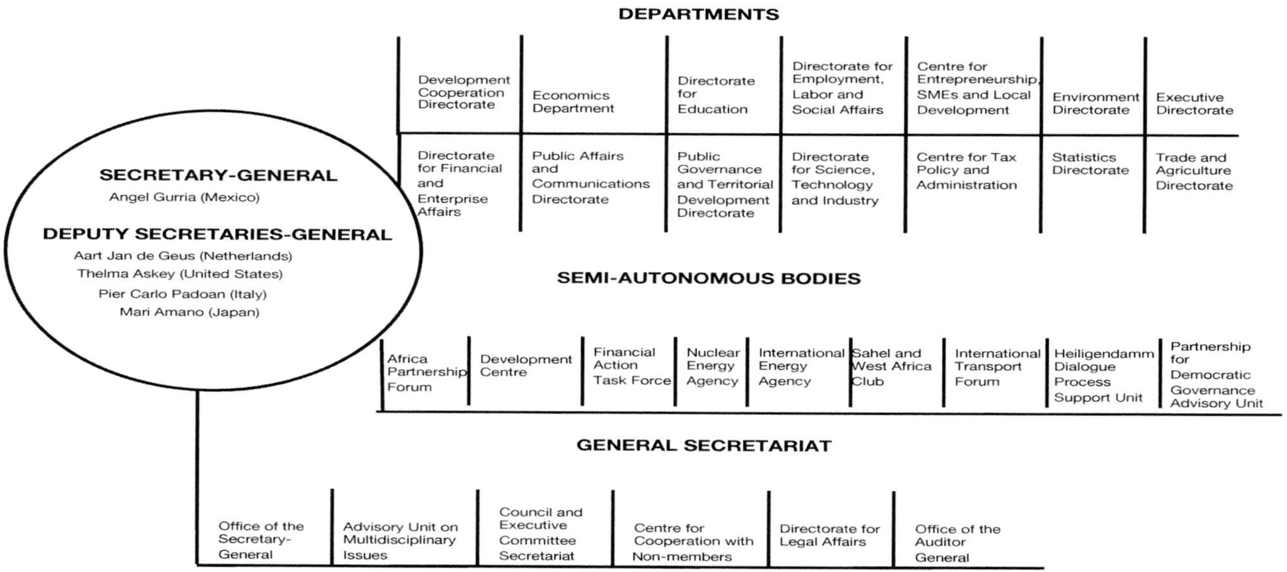

SECRETARY-GENERAL
Angel Gurria (Mexico)

DEPUTY SECRETARIES-GENERAL
Aart Jan de Geus (Netherlands)
Thelma Askey (United States)
Pier Carlo Padoan (Italy)
Mari Amano (Japan)

DEPARTMENTS

- Development Cooperation Directorate
  - Directorate for Financial and Enterprise Affairs
- Economics Department
  - Public Affairs and Communications Directorate
- Directorate for Education
  - Public Governance and Territorial Development Directorate
- Directorate for Employment, Labor and Social Affairs
  - Directorate for Science, Technology and Industry
- Centre for Entrepreneurship, SMEs and Local Development
  - Centre for Tax Policy and Administration
- Environment Directorate
  - Statistics Directorate
- Executive Directorate
  - Trade and Agriculture Directorate

SEMI-AUTONOMOUS BODIES

- Africa Partnership Forum
- Development Centre
- Financial Action Task Force
- Nuclear Energy Agency
- International Energy Agency
- Sahel and West Africa Club
- International Transport Forum
- Heiligendamm Dialogue Process Support Unit
- Partnership for Democratic Governance Advisory Unit

GENERAL SECRETARIAT

- Office of the Secretary-General
- Advisory Unit on Multidisciplinary Issues
- Council and Executive Committee Secretariat
- Centre for Cooperation with Non-members
- Directorate for Legal Affairs
- Office of the Auditor General

Figure 2.2 OECD organization chart
Source: OECD, *Annual Report 2008* (Paris: OECD, 2008), 110–1.

Committees

Instructed by the Council to study specific questions (Rule 22a) committees are the place where the secretariat exposes its dispassionate analysis to political realities and the OECD produces the policy advice and, subject to council ratification, the "soft law" instruments for which it is famed. As custodians of the organization's cherished peer review processes, committees also take the lead in monitoring the enactment of OECD instruments. Currently there are over 260 OECD committees, working groups and expert groups (see Table 2.4). The majority of these bodies entitle all OECD countries and selected non-OECD countries and organizations to membership. That said, some smaller, less developed OECD members opt out of bodies that are inconsequential to their interests or where they lack suitable personnel.

Table 2.4 OECD committees by directorate (July 2008)

Directorate	Main committees	Sub-groups	Total
Centre for Entrepreneurship, SMEs and Local Development	2	1	3
Centre for Tax Policy and Administration	2	19	21
Development Co-operation Directorate	1	8	9
Directorate for Education	5	14	19
Directorate for Employment, Labour and Social Affairs	2	14	16
Directorate for Financial and Enterprise Affairs	5	19	24
Directorate for Science, Technology and Industry	6	17	23
Economics Department	2	3	5
Environment Directorate	2	24	26
General Secretariat	2	21	23
Inter-organization Study Section on Salaries and Prices	1	0	1
International Energy Agency	1	13	14
OECD Nuclear Energy Agency	1	31	32
Public Governance and Territorial Development Directorate	3	13	16
Sahel and West Africa Club	1	0	1
Statistics Directorate	1	4	5
Trade and Agriculture Directorate	4	21	25
Total	41	222	263

Source: OECD, "On-Line Guide to OECD Intergovernmental Activity," available at http://www2.oecd.org/oecdgroups (Accessed 1 July 2008).

So, while Spain, the Netherlands, Sweden, Belgium, Austria, Switzerland, and the G8 countries belong to over 230 OECD bodies, Poland and Iceland are members of only 178 and 193 respectively.[10] Within bounds set by the Council, OECD committees may delve into any question within their competence (Rule 22b) and have license to customize their working routines and relationships with non-member representatives. Hence committees are versatile and what follows are general rules of thumb about their composition, structure, and relationship with other branches of the organization. Most directorates have one or more substantive committees whose members rally to, petition for, or contribute to, work by the secretariat or review developments in a broad policy area. Committees may establish subsidiary working parties and expert groups to facilitate their work (Rule 21b). These bodies tend to evaluate obscure or nettlesome puzzles to avoid overloading or sabotaging the headline committee's progress. For example, the two foremost committees of the Environment Directorate are the Environmental Policy Committee (EPOC) and the Chemicals Committee. In turn, the EPOC has 18 auxiliary groups dealing, inter alia, with trade, taxation, agricultural aspects of environmental policies, biodiversity, waste prevention, transport, chemicals, pesticides, biotechnology, pollution, and good laboratory practices. The Chemicals Committee has six task forces and working parties reconnoitering existing and new chemicals, biocides, nanomaterials, and harmonizing classification and labeling.

Intermittently, OECD committees meet in ministerial session to launch, give impetus to, or conclude a major project. Usually, however, committees are composed of representatives of the OECD secretariat, members of permanent delegations, senior officials and connoisseurs nominated by member governments and international organizations and, increasingly, dignitaries from non-member governments and civil society. Every year 40,000 delegates attend OECD committees in Paris[11] and over 16,000 officials in 2,000 ministries now enroll to OLISnet, a restricted online portal providing remote access to committee information and discussion groups where they can mingle with the secretariat and their counterparts abroad.[12] As previously mentioned, both real and "virtual" OECD committees operate in privacy to encourage the exchange of forthright opinions. That the secretariat and national officials work in tandem in OECD bodies is significant. OECD bodies bind the brightest folk working in a given policy area together into transgovernmental networks of knowledge-based experts. These specialists affect national and international policymaking by using their superior knowledge to frame for decision-makers the nature of policy problems and the best means to cope with them.

Non-members and civil society

As part of its outreach strategy, the OECD is taking steps to con-solidate and diversify relations with non-members and civil society (see Chapters 1 and 5). Their exclusion from the Council means non-members cannot mold the OECD's inherent agenda but they can nudge it through immersion in the organization's committees and sub-sidiary bodies. Non-members (states, international organizations, and civil society) participate in OECD bodies according to preconditions set by the council (Article 12, Rule 9). Rather than confer observer status on an organization-wide basis the OECD invites non-members to become associated with selected subsidiary bodies at one of three levels. The lowest level is ad hoc invitations to individual meetings where non-members merely contribute to preliminary discussions. The intermediate level is "regular observer." Subsidiary bodies invite reg-ular observers to more of their meetings and the expectation is that they will actively contribute to the work of the body and make a financial recompense to the OECD. Regular observers can be barred from all or part of a subsidiary body's meetings (Rule 9b), may only report to the meeting with the chair's assent (Rule 9c), and are not embroiled in or bound by the body's decisions. The final level is "full participation." Though the council can adjourn or terminate such arrangements, the OECD offers full participation for indefinite periods and non-members assume rights and responsibilities equivalent to OECD members belonging to the same body. Non-members must adopt and adhere to OECD instruments promulgated by the body concerned, participate in its peer review and surveillance processes, and pay their dues under the Part II budget.[13]

This stratified approach and latitude of committees to determine collusions with non-members produces a kaleidoscope of relationships between the OECD and non-members. Presently 69 non-member countries observe one or more subsidiary body (see Table 2.5) but 10 countries account for 70 percent of those relationships. Similarly, 101 international organizations are OECD observers but the World Bank (observer in 45 bodies), the IMF (39), the WTO (18), the Coun-cil of Europe (17), the WHO (16), the BIS (9), and numerous UN bodies (72) account for the majority.[14] Additionally, non-member access is uneven across the OECD. Much non-member activity is con-centrated in peripheral committees such as those dealing with agri-culture, but the OECD restricts access to its innermost economic bodies to a handful of international organizations and systemically significant economies.

Table 2.5 Participation by non-member states in OECD bodies (June 2008)

Non-member	Observer	Full participant	Total
Russian Federation	74	9	83
Chile	60	12	72
Israel	52	14	66
Slovenia	48	16	64
South Africa	40	16	56
Brazil	43	12	55
Argentina	26	9	35
China	32	2	34
Estonia	21	10	31
India	26	2	28
Romania	6	16	22
Ukraine	12	3	15
Bulgaria	2	12	14
Lithuania	5	8	13
Egypt	6	7	13
Morocco	4	8	12
Singapore	10	0	10
Hong Kong	8	1	9
Croatia	0	8	8
Latvia	1	6	7
Serbia	0	7	7
Bolivia	0	6	6
Montenegro	0	6	6
Uganda	0	6	6
Chinese Taipei	5	0	5
Indonesia	3	2	5
Uruguay	0	5	5
Other	5	62	67
Total	489	265	754

Source: OECD, "On-Line Guide to OECD Intergovernmental Activity," available at http://www2.oecd.org/oecdgroups/ (Accessed 30 June 2008); OECD, *The OECD's Global Relations Programme 2007–08* (Paris: OECD, 2007), 18–23.

A similar pattern emerges with civil society where TUAC, the OECD's "interface for labor unions,"[15] and BIAC, "the voice of OECD business,"[16] retain a privileged position. Financed and steered by affiliates in OECD states, BIAC and TUAC are autonomous organizations that exist to sway OECD policy and inform members about the repercussions of its work. TUAC's register encompasses 58 labor unions with 66 million members while BIAC's entourage entails 39 business peak groups representing 8 million companies.[17] Distinguishing BIAC and TUAC from other civil society actors is the breadth and depth of their assimilation into OECD work. Mostly the OECD engages civil society on single issues in a narrow range of bodies, but TUAC and BIAC's linkages are institutionalized and widespread. BIAC and TUAC are the only civil society actors to have permanent, if tiny, secretariats in Paris taking advantage of their propinquity to lobby permanent delegations and OECD personnel. Complementing this are the numerous TUAC and BIAC nominees who visit fleetingly to participate in subsidiary bodies of the OECD. BIAC and TUAC have a ritual dialogue with the OECD through the Liaison Committee (of the Council) with International Non-Governmental Organizations which is chaired by the Secretary-General, make submissions to the MCM, and have separate annual audiences with senior OECD staff. Nevertheless, telling interventions by BIAC, TUAC and other civil society organizations to flagship OECD policies are sparse.

Putting it all together: the OECD's way of working

The variable geometry and enfranchisement of OECD bodies to determine their working routines allow variation in the organization's policy processes. Nonetheless, the OECD's policy cycle tends to imitate that portrayed in Figure 2.3. Once the decision is taken to stalk a policy problem at the OECD, the next step is to collect the requisite data. Recall that Article 3(a) obliges members to supply the OECD "with the information necessary for the accomplishment of its tasks." Information takes a variety of forms, from regularized statistical returns to more abstract qualitative data detailing the experiences, ideas, and opinions of national policymakers. Stage two sees the secretariat sift the data and crunch the numbers to identify trends, correlations and causations, test hypotheses, and zoom in on areas of consensus and controversy. The research illuminates evidence to support, refine or debunk prevailing mindsets and the secretariat may devise conceptual apparatus to help national officials clarify the precise nature of the issues for discussion in OECD committees and working groups.

These discussions are the third phase of the OECD work cycle. Using the secretariat's commentary and analysis as a point of departure, participants congregate in OECD committees and working groups to exchange information and ideas about their own experiences and explicate their stance and ramifications for their economy or society. This can be a protracted, iterative process requiring additional research by the secretariat to propel the debate. Successful discussions will foster cognizance of other national positions and lead to converging knowledge and analysis of the issue amongst officials from

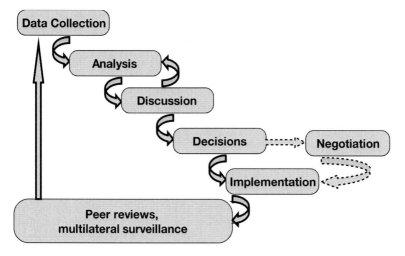

Figure 2.3 The OECD's way of working
Source: adapted from OECD, *Organisation for the Economic Cooperation and Development,*available at http://oecd.org/dataoecd/29/28/2397890.ppt (Accessed 7 August 2007).

different national capitals. By this point, the topic should be sufficiently clear for states to define their national position and move to the decisions stage of the policy cycle by proposing solutions and standards of best practice for the policy problem in question. Each year the OECD publishes more than 200 reports summarizing these decisions and imploring contracted parties to employ them. Sporadically, countries take decisions one stage further, using the consensus reached as a springboard to negotiate a legally codified instrument for adoption by the council. The expectation is that states will then implement these pledges whether formalized or not. The incentive for doing so rests not on prescribed sanctions but the awareness that their peers are watching. Multilateral surveillance is the cornerstone of the OECD method, epitomized by the pervasive peer review process.[18] Peer reviews are meticulous evaluations of a country's (or group of countries') performance in a stated area by other countries. They gauge the extent to which states comply with best practices exalted at the OECD and recommend policies to address deficiencies. As well as their monitoring role, peer reviews are imperative for closing the OECD policy loop. Peer reviews yield new data about policies that work, stimulating fresh analysis and discussion and laying the foundations for future guidelines and standards.

There is no standard template for an OECD peer review, but there are structural and procedural commonalities. Structurally all peer review processes have a protocol stipulating who and what will be reviewed, how often and by whom. Peer reviews occur as part of the perennial surveillance practices of OECD bodies, but are sometimes intrinsic to validating the application of legal instruments such as the Convention on Combating Bribery of Foreign Public Officials in International Business Transactions. Peer reviews possess settled benchmarks against which to measure a country's record and actors elected to undertake the appraisal. In terms of the actors, most peer reviews are concerted efforts between officials of the secretariat, the country under review, and other members of the relevant OECD body. Typically, to prune the process, committees designate a couple of countries to pilot the preliminary phases of a review but include all countries in the final stages. Finally, review processes have techniques for fashioning and disseminating the results of the process. The OECD ordinarily publishes the outcomes of peer reviews for public consumption. The length of peer review cycles fluctuates across the organization. Peer reviews of economic policies, the *Economic Surveys* (see Box 2.1), occur biennially, whereas those of environmental policies happen every five to seven years.[19]

Procedurally, peer reviews have three phases. Phase one is preparatory, with the OECD secretariat garnering background data and the country under review assessing its own performance. Phase two is consultative with a team from the secretariat and lead review countries conducting a scrupulous discourse with government officials and specialists from civil society and academic organizations.[20] The review team prepares a draft report for the last phase of the process, the assessment phase. Here a delegation from the country under review comes before a plenary session of the applicable OECD body to discuss the draft report and defend its position against well briefed inquisitors. Through these discussions, participants hammer out an agreed document released into the public domain.

Box 2.1: OECD *Economic Surveys*

The *Economic Surveys* merit special attention because they are amongst the most cited OECD outputs and represent the culmination of the oldest OECD peer review process since emulated by other directorates. The OECD supervises *Economic Surveys* through the Economics Department (ECO) and, more specifically, the Economic and Development Review Committee (EDRC). An *Economic Survey* aims to advertise insights into the policy challenges and economic standing of individual countries, enhance national and international economic policy debates, evaluate each country's performance against OECD macroeconomic and structural policy yardsticks, identify frailties, and recommend therapies to deliver sustainable long-term economic growth. With two exceptions, the recipe for conducting *Economic Surveys* has barely altered. Originally the EDRC examined the economic policies of member states on an annual basis. The enlargement of the OECD and rolling out the peer review process to certain non-members (Brazil, India, Chile, China, South Africa, Indonesia, and the Russian Federation) means that today intervals of up to two years elapse between appraisals. The other change is the weight given to structural policies. Reviews once focused on short-run macroeconomic trends, but by the 1980s structural policies and their interrelationship with macroeconomic affairs were staple components of the *Economic Surveys*.

The preparatory phase of the *Economic Survey* sees a country desk in ECO amass background information about the country under review. National officials complete a questionnaire issued by ECO in which they detail contemporary and forthcoming economic developments and policies and the roots of their suppositions. To solicit further information and refine the verdicts in the questionnaire, a diminutive delegation from ECO makes rendezvous with high-ranking bureaucrats from the central bank, economic ministries and a variety of experts and social partners in the country concerned. The findings provide the material for a draft report by the secretariat which is accessible through OLISnet. This marks the start of the peer review's consultative phase. Interested parties peruse the draft and the country under review prepares a rejoinder ahead of a follow-up visit from ECO staff. This expedition enables the secretariat to renew the original data and trigger discussions on infirmities inferred by the draft survey. This consultative phase ends with a convocation of OECD staff and senior officials (and sometimes ministers) before the ECO outfit withdraws to Paris to compile the final draft survey.

The evaluative phase of the process embarks with the circulation of the draft survey and, about four weeks later, a day-long plenary session of the EDRC where a delegation of around a dozen representatives from the country under review submit themselves to interrogation by their EDRC peers. All 30

OECD members, plus the European Commission, belong to the EDRC while the BIS, IMF, WTO, World Bank, and EFTA are regular observers. The Russian Federation is also a regular observer but only participates with the permission of the country under review. The themes to be broached and the bearings of the discussion are primed by a "Questions for Discussion Note" jointly contrived by the secretariat and officials from the two countries handpicked by the EDRC as lead reviewers. The meeting commences with testimony by the country under review rehearsing points of dispute with the draft survey and justifying policy choices. Delegates from lead review countries then have the opportunity to cross-examine the team from the country under review before the floor is opened to probes from the remaining committee members. Once the discussion has run its course, the chair summarizes the meeting and stresses revisions for inclusion in the final survey. The following day the team from the country under review thrashes out with the secretariat a version of the document that they are happy to see published. Generally revisions are minor, and involve expunging politically sensitive advice. This is because the report must be approved unanimously and members are unlikely to brook a report that ignores their collective advice. Once the report is approved it is published under EDRC auspices and made available to the public.

(*Sources*: OECD, *Peer Review: a Tool for Co-operation and Change* (Paris: OECD, 2007), 4–5; Fabrizio Pagani, *Peer Review: A Tool for Co-operation and Change: An Analysis of an OECD Working Method* (Paris: OECD, 2002), 22–24; Armin Schafer, "A New Form of Governance? Comparing the Open Method of Co-ordination to Multilateral Surveillance by the IMF and the OECD," *Journal of European Public Policy* 13, no. 1 (January 2006): 73–75.)

Conclusion

Chapter 1 made a number of claims about the deeds of the OECD. This chapter has sought to explain how the OECD works toward achieving these outcomes by examining the role and function of the organization's bodies, their input to the OECD policy cycle and the peer review process. Several themes recur throughout this chapter. First, whatever the guile of the Secretary-General and the precociousness of the secretariat, the OECD is piloted by the members. They are the gatekeepers for the issues that enter the organization, they hold the purse strings, and their representatives far outnumber those of the OECD. Nevertheless—to reinforce one of the messages of Chapter 1— the absence of senior ministerial figures from the MCM suggests some larger states are now setting less store by the OECD and choosing alternative forums in which to prosecute their cooperative ventures. Next, although it is possible to discern the contours of an OECD method, the OECD is an enormously diverse institution. As we will see in greater detail in Chapter 5, while some parts of the organization are quite gregarious and extend a hand to non-members and civil society, others, notably the economic committees where most is at stake, are introverted and opaque. Lastly, this chapter hints at the scale of OECD activity. With 40,000 visitors to over 260 committees and working groups spread across 17 policy directorates, the OECD has one of the most hectic schedules of all international economic organizations. To recap, we now have an almanac of OECD accomplishments and an account of how the organization goes about its tasks. However, the book now turns to the ticklish question posed in the book's introduction, that is *why* an organization with no official system of rewards and sanctions and whose methods are primarily consultative can wield influence in global governance. The next chapter etches a framework for understanding the contribution that the OECD and the activity therein makes to global governance.

3 A framework for understanding

The OECD operates across a battery of policy areas and employs a variety of policy processes. However, the "kind of influence the organization exerts and the way it does so are little discussed and there is little scholarly literature about it."[1] This chapter elaborates a four-dimensional framework for understanding the OECD's place in, and influence over, global governance. The model expounds upon what the OECD stands for, the objects that alter as a consequence of deliberations at the OECD, and how the organization promotes international cooperation to swell our capacity to manage our global affairs.

The first dimension, cognitive governance, refers to the OECD as the personification of a community of nations grounded in the belief that capitalist and democratic modes of governance are the optimum means of managing our collective affairs. The second dimension, normative governance, refers to the generation of shared knowledge and expected standards of behavior amongst those involved in OECD bodies and the bearing this has upon national and international policymaking. Evaluating the organization's impact in this regard is something of a minefield as the purpose of OECD meetings is to consult and advise rather than issue directives. The parsimonious language of international diplomacy produces guidance and commitments susceptible to differing interpretations, making precise correlations between the OECD's counsel and national economic policies difficult to ascertain. Moreover, disentangling the OECD's influence from the many other drivers of norms and ideas would require a forensic examination of individual policy areas over a number of years. Nevertheless, this chapter will suggest there is some evidence to support assertions that the OECD's ideas leach over a long period into national and international policymaking. The majority of OECD work remains consultative, but occasionally OECD members sanctify their consensus to give it additional moral force. The third, legal, dimension of OECD governance refers to the passage of international law through the OECD Council. Predominantly the OECD produces "soft law" enforced through surveillance and peer review. The final dimension, palliative governance, sees the OECD as the masseur in global governance, dealing with difficult or neglected problems and drawing the sting from conflicts in other global institutions.

Cognitive governance

Cognitive governance refers to the OECD's capacity to engender and reproduce a sense of identity and community amongst its members by engineering and propagating a set of values, perspectives, expectations, and discourses about their place and that of the organization in the global polity.[2] Specifically, joining the OECD "reflects the respective country's wish to establish itself as a member of a community of nations committed to democratic as well as market-oriented institutions."[3]

Throughout its first three decades, the OECD community developed as part of the Cold War landscape. For what was a primarily transatlantic organization, faster economic growth through cooperation helped underpin the military deterrent needed to repel the common threat posed to many OECD members by the Soviet Union. During the Cold War many, not least the secretaries-general of the organization, viewed the OECD as an integral branch of the Western economic and security framework developed after the Second World War.[4] The OECD's depiction of itself "as an economic counterpart to NATO"[5] is overblown, however. Many OECD countries, including Sweden, Finland, Austria, Switzerland, Spain (until 1982), France (episodically), and the organization's non-European members did not belong to NATO. Furthermore, if the OECD was purely a Cold War combatant presumably it would have vanished at the Cold War's denouement.

The significance of the Cold War for the OECD lay not in a faceoff between two military alliances but the political and economic ideas they stood for. The OECD "symbolized a consensus about the superiority of capitalism and democracy as the organizing principles for global governance."[6] All countries that had a demonstrable commitment to working toward a market economy and pluralist democracy were eligible for OECD membership. Gradually this community and the countries therein, especially when their levels of prosperity began to surge ahead of communist regimes with centrally planned economies, came to be seen as the prototype for the best kinds of state in the modern global system. As early as 1964 the Japanese prime minister suggested that upon accession to the OECD his country "joined the advanced international community both in name and in fact."[7] The democratic and economic transitions of much of the former communist bloc, and China's—albeit quirky—embrace of capitalist tenets suggests the OECD's official history is right to claim that it "stood as a colossal, and colossally successful, challenge to Soviet and Chinese communism."[8] The apparent triumph of OECD values paradoxically produced a temporary outbreak of schizophrenia within the organization. With free markets and pluralist political systems spreading into Eastern Europe, Asia, and Latin America, the OECD community was less distinct than heretofore. Nevertheless, it quickly became clear that declarations of the "end of history,"[9] where democratic and market institutions swept all before them, were premature. Before the end of the decade global capitalist institutions were under siege from anti-globalization protestors and, in many countries, promised democratic transitions never materialized. If anything, the OECD community has become more cohesive and the OECD a more militant promoter of democratic and free market principles since the end of the Cold War. The thawing of relations between East and West means the OECD no longer has to tolerate undemocratic members because of overriding security concerns. Writing in 1991, then Secretary-General Jean-Claude Paye noted the OECD "is the only international organization of which it can be said that it comprises almost all the developed, pluralist democracy, market economy countries, and *only* such countries."[10] Strictly speaking there is nothing in the OECD Convention that says prospective members *must* be market-democracies, but the organization has made it clear that countries that do not meet these criteria will not gain accession (see Chapter 5). Because the OECD is viewed as the "advanced international community" the organization does, similarly to the EU, dangle membership as a means of encouraging capitalist and democratic reforms in non-member countries. In other words, the OECD is important for what it is as much as what it does.

Normative governance

Normative governance, the advancement of cooperation through the dissemination of convergent knowledge and ideas through recurrent OECD meetings, is the most elusive but doubtless most important element of the four-dimensional model. Article 3(b) of the OECD Convention requires members to "consult together on a continuing basis." OECD committees and working groups are the main medium for these consultations. As Chapter 2 describes, these bodies customarily throw together near identical conclaves of senior policymakers to exchange information and discuss and review policies in discrete areas. Through these consultations participants learn from and about each other, coming to share perspectives on the world and superior ways of navigating given problems. Indeed, as Robert Wolfe intones, possibly "the most important thing that changes because of the OECD might be the thinking of the people involved."[11] This changed thinking seeps into wider policymaking circles when officials return to their homeland armed with ideas agreed with, or pilfered from, their counterparts. These ideas gain traction in national capitals and other international organizations owing to the acknowledged expertise of those involved in OECD work. To borrow a phrase, the OECD generates "international incentives for national policymaking."[12] Not only might it be argued that officials and the governments they advise would be brave or foolhardy to abjure knowledge excavated from the collective experiences of 30 likeminded partners, officials visiting the OECD also know that the organization will be monitoring the extent to which agreed positions are being implemented, and may one day have to defend their record in the context of a peer review. This motivates officials to advocate agreed positions in national capitals to avoid a loss of reputation amongst their peers.

Before going on to examine how and why the knowledge gleaned by participants in OECD activities influences national and international policymaking, it is necessary to establish the kinds of knowledge generated. Per-Olof Busch suggests the OECD yields three overlapping categories of collective intelligence.[13] The first, "informatory knowledge,"[14] refers to the hoards of data accumulated by OECD research and which is stored in, and dispersed through, policy inventories and statistical databases. The OECD presently curates some 40 databases exhaustively chronicling past, present, and projected statistics for 26 broad subject areas.[15]

A drought of precise and authoritative information often sounds the death knell for international cooperation. Hence, the OECD's capacities to beget datasets for previously untouched issues and internationally standardized methodologies to render data more complete, reliable, and internationally comparable are valuable assets. For example, the OECD's System of National Accounts (SNA) (first developed in 1968 and jointly revised with the IMF, European Commission and World Bank in 1993) is a scaffold of "internationally agreed concepts, definitions, classifications and accounting rules"[16] on which countries construct many macroeconomic measures including GDP, and levels of investment, consumption, and government indebtedness. The SNA ensures that while countries use dissimilar terminology and define some variables slightly differently, their national accounting aggregates are cross-nationally equivalent and fuel cooperative ventures. In the aftermath of the Asian financial crises in 1997–98 for instance, the U.S. Federal Reserve's decision to inject liquidity into the international financial system

> depended for its timeliness and effectiveness on the reliability and transparency of the economic and financial information upon which the policymakers based their judgments ... it should be clear that the availability of international comparable and consistent data on macroeconomic, financial and trade performance was a tribute to the accomplishments of the OECD.[17]

The second category, "conceptual knowledge," comprises the development of common prisms through which OECD policymakers peer upon certain problems and understand how the world works. This includes the evolution of shared benchmarks and tools for conceiving, checking, and calculating the impact of specific policies, communal language and concepts, and agreement over causal relationships. A good illustration is the Environment Directorate's "Pressure-State-Response" (PSR) model used by the OECD and its members to structure work on the reporting, development, and inspection of environmental policies. As the name implies, the PSR model has indicators to measure the "pressure" human activity places on the environment, the present "state" of the environment, natural resources, and key eco-systems, and the policy and behavioral "response" of societies to alleviate environmental degradation. The framework is deliberately abstract to encourage policymakers to see the big picture, in particular to highlight linkages between environmental and other policy domains.[18] The model is used by the OECD Secretariat to identify salient indicators and structure the Environmental Performance Reviews and is widely invoked (sometimes in a slightly adapted form) by domestic ministries preparing reports tracking their own environmental progress and performance. Indeed some states, Australia for example, have used the PSR framework to standardize the countrywide reporting practices of sub-national governments.

The final category, "analytical knowledge,"[19] refers to collective wisdom about the best policies to tackle problems. Ultimately the entire OECD process from the initial research, the conduct of national and local case studies, onsite visits, and monitoring and peer review is geared, to quote the OECD Convention, to "promote policies designed" to meet the shared objectives of member states. Because OECD members share similar objectives and understandings about the world, "it is highly probable that what works, or fails, in one industrial country will have similar effects in another."[20] In other words, through interactions at the OECD, states learn from each other about policies that work and which the organization distills into its reports and peer reviews in the form of policy advice. As their country regularly tops the OECD's PISA survey, Finnish schoolchildren are accustomed to swarms of foreign visitors to their classrooms rummaging for tips to improve their own education systems.[21] This does not mean states slavishly impersonate the policies of others or the paradigms emitting from OECD reports. For the most part states siphon off aspects of the OECD's advice that they find useful and adapt it to their domestic context. The policies of states are not necessarily being harmonized as a consequence of their involvement with the OECD, but are converging on similar generic models underpinned by shared analysis of the conundrums at hand. In short, through this analytical convergence the OECD may not change what countries strive for but does change how they try to attain it.

The next mystery surrounds *why* the OECD is able to sway policy debates. The OECD has no financial or formal legal resources to bring to bear and so relies instead on authoritative and moral resources. The organization's authority derives from the exceptional talents of the secretariat and the national officials delegated to OECD committees and working groups. These skilful and creative individuals are highly respected experts in their chosen field who, through constantly considering policy problems with their peers, have knowledge that outsiders lack. This knowledge translates into power when officials return to national capitals because they have superior information to prevail over colleagues favoring alternative approaches and can frame policies in a manner intelligible to their political taskmasters.

This deference to "experts" contributes to another source of authority, namely the OECD's reputation as an impartial observer of global events. This is not to say there is no such thing as an OECD view or that it does not peddle prescriptions permeated by specific ideologies, but that many view the organization as an "authoritative source of independent data."[22] In a congested market place for information and ideas, those stamped with the OECD imprimatur are seldom, if ever, accused of bias or political manipulation. Without feeling the need to justify it, politicians, bureaucrats, interest groups, the media, and the general citizenry capitalize upon the OECD's outputs to leverage domestic debates or win support for unpopular measures. The OECD is most likely to hit the headlines "when the policy-makers, desiring to bolster their case before parliaments and the public, stress the foreign policy aspects and refer to OECD discussions as evidence."[23] In 2005, for example, the Belgian government invoked OECD research on ageing societies to push through detested reforms to the social security system.[24]

Members can deliberately sponsor work at the OECD to further a domestic agenda. The Japanese Environment Agency patronized OECD work on extended producer responsibility (the extent to which producers should be answerable for the post-consumption effects of their merchandise) not only to understand how others were dealing with the issue but also to bolster the agenda they were pushing domestically.[25] Critics commandeer downbeat OECD reports to discredit government policies and petition for reform. In September 2008, the OECD stoked a political rumpus in the U.K. when its interim economic outlook suggested that the U.K. economy was the worst placed amongst the G7 to withstand the projected global economic downturn. Overall, relations between the OECD and member states are like a patient listening to the diagnosis and course of treatment recommended by their physician. Patients may loathe what they hear and ignore the injunctions, but they do not challenge the doctor's verdict or the techniques through which it was reached.

The organization's moral wherewithal arises from peer pressure effected through OECD bodies. OECD bodies summon the same officials who, over time, build up personal amities and may come to identify more with their international peer group than their counterparts at home. Participants in OECD bodies feel they ought to follow prescriptions agreed with their peers to avoid a loss of credibility, especially as they are conscious that OECD bodies are continually assessing compliance through monitoring and peer review.[26] Peer review is the most overt way the OECD exerts peer pressure. Several international organizations utilize peer reviews but the novelties of the OECD's processes are their intensity and levels of ownership by national officials. The OECD's *Economic Surveys* intimately involve national officials throughout the peer review process, culminating, even for the smallest states, in a day-long grilling in the EDRC (see Box 2.1). In contrast, the IMF's Executive Board considers country reports in a couple of hours, typically in the absence of policymakers from the country concerned.[27] Reports "name and shame" states that are not complying with agreed positions or who are performing poorly in relation to preset standards which, as previously suggested, have the potential to stir up a hornet's nest in national capitals.

Friendships built though OECD bodies can avert combustible international situations. As Keohane and Nye suggested in their seminal article on transgovernmental relations, the "regularized patterns of policy coordination can. ... create attitudes and relationships that will at least marginally change policy or affect its implementation."[28] Knowing that the next meeting with their peers is proximate deters cheating and "a continuous awareness of the foreign impact of a country's policies can suffuse future policy choices and reduce the danger of actions inimical to the interests of others."[29] The policy advice given to governments by officials involved in OECD networks is tinted by their comprehension of the problems confronting their foreign contemporaries and prognostication about their probable response. Consequently it is plausible that states will, even if inadvertently, produce more compatible international outcomes than they otherwise would. Furthermore, in cases where rogue countries are not toeing the agreed line they can explain their reasons in frank but private exchanges with their peers. While this may not lead to the convergence of national policies, it may lead to "informed divergence,"[30] with governments reluctantly accepting exemptions to agreed positions afflicting one party without risking a public spat.

As the opening section of this chapter stated, exactly how much impact peer reviews and peer pressure have upon states is a thornier issue. The OECD naturally suggests that peer pressure "is a means of soft persuasion which can become an important driving force to stimulate the State to change, achieve goals and meet standards."[31] There is some evidence to verify this assertion, but confidential interviews and publications by those involved with the organization's work are wispier when it comes to stating policy changes that have occurred directly as a consequence of the OECD, and there are limits to OECD influence.

First, although OECD discussions might help reshape or soften national interests, ultimately it cannot trump them. OECD advice falls on stony ground wherever it runs contrary to the interests of key states or they lack the political will to promote it. An anonymous contributor to an early edition of the *OECD Observer* noted that the OECD method "does not inevitably lead to co-ordination; even when it does, that co-ordination may still be inadequate, fragmentary or belated ... more rigorous methods of international cooperation and co-ordination can easily be imagined. But national sovereignty remains an inescapable fact."[32] Second, and relatedly, while countries address items jointly at the OECD they do not do so equally. The OECD's advice resonates less in Washington and London than it does in Reykjavik and Oslo. States with sophisticated infrastructures and larger pools of domestic expertise are better placed to refute criticisms made during a peer review. Whereas the OECD's June 2005 *Economic Outlook* recommended cuts in interest rates by the European Central Bank, this plea was not replicated in the organization's *Economic Survey* of the euro area published a month later. This did not reflect a sudden change of heart by the OECD secretariat but the fact that the *Economic Outlook* is written solely by the OECD staff whereas the various European institutions can call for changes to the *Economic Survey* before it is published.[33] Third, the debates sparked by the OECD tend to be ephemeral. The OECD's 2008 report on the U.K. economy rapidly disappeared from the public radar and seemingly made scant difference to the economic policies of Gordon Brown's administration.

Legal governance

Ordinarily, OECD activity goes no further than the consultative behavior described in the previous section. Sometimes, however, states do codify consensual knowledge into legal texts. The legal dimension of OECD governance, "the capacity of the OECD Member States to adopt decisions and international agreements within the framework of the Council,"[34] takes a number of forms (see Table 3.1).

OECD Decisions are the most formal which, unless they abstain when it is adopted, "shall be binding on all the Members."[35] Strictly speaking OECD Decisions are not international treaties but "they do entail, for Member countries, the same kind of legal obligations as those subscribed to under international treaties."[36] Signatories do not have a choice about whether to implement a decision but have some leeway to decide when and how it is incorporated into national law.[37] Recommendations of the OECD are "submitted to the Members for consideration in order that they may, if they consider it opportune, provide for their implementation."[38] By far the most numerous of OECD Acts (see Table 3.1), recommendations "are not legally binding, but practice accords them great moral force as representing the political will of Member countries and there is an expectation that Member countries will do their utmost to fully implement a Recommendation."[39] For this reason, members tend to signal their intention not to implement a recommendation by abstaining, as Switzerland and Luxembourg did in regard to the Recommendation to Counter Harmful Tax Competition in 1998.

Decisions and recommendations together account for over 80 percent of legal governance, with the remainder coming in the form of

Table 3.1 Compendium of OECD Acts (July 2008)

	Decisions	Recommendations	Others	Total
Agriculture	4	4	0	8
Anti-corruption	1	3	3	7
Capital movements	1	0	0	1
Competition law and policy	0	10	0	10
Consumer policy	1	9	0	10
Corporate governance	0	1	1	2
Current invisibles operations	1	1	0	2
Development assistance	0	3	4	7
Education	0	2	1	3
Employment, labor and social affairs	0	2	2	4
Energy	1	0	0	1
Environment	15	51	4	70
Financial markets	0	7	0	7
Fiscal affairs	0	16	1	17
Information, computer and communications policy	0	9	5	14
Insurance	1	13	0	14
International investment and multinational enterprises	4	8	4	16
Nuclear energy	1	4	3	8
Public management	0	3	0	3
Scientific and technological policy	0	6	5	11
Shipbuilding and maritime transport	0	2	4	6
Steel	0	0	1	1
Tourism	1	2	0	3
Trade	0	4	2	6
Total	31	160	40	231

Source: OECD, "Instruments of the OECD by Subject," available at www.olis.
oecd.org/horizontal/oecdacts.nsf/subject?OpenView&Start=1&Count=1000&
ExpandView (Accessed 1 July 2008). These 'other' OECD Acts include
Agreements, Arrangements, Conventions, DAC Recommendations,
Declarations, Guidelines, and Understandings.

Agreements, Conventions, Declarations, and Arrangements or Understandings. Agreements and conventions are legally binding instruments
concluded within the OECD Council. The latter are freestanding
agreements to which some non-members belong, for example the anti-
bribery convention. In contrast, arrangements, understandings, and
declarations are neither formal OECD Acts nor legally binding.
Nevertheless, "they are noted by the OECD Council and their application is generally monitored by the responsible OECD body."[40] What

differentiates them is that declarations are "solemn texts setting out relatively precise policy commitments subscribed to by the governments of Member countries,"[41] whereas arrangements and understandings are "instruments, negotiated and adopted within the framework of the Organisation by *some* Member countries."[42] Uniting these various OECD Acts is that they are all "soft" as opposed to "hard" law. Hard law

> refers to legally binding obligations that are precise (or can be made precise through adjudication or the issuance of detailed regulations) and that delegate authority for interpreting and implementing the law ... the realm of "soft law" begins once legal arrangements are weakened along one or more of the dimensions of obligation, precision, and delegation.[43]

The OECD's legal arrangements are diluted along all three axes. Rather than elucidating precise obligations, OECD Acts commit states to general standards of righteous behavior or principles of best practice to follow when transposing OECD acts into national law and policy-making. For instance, rather than expounding a detailed regulatory framework, the OECD's Principles of Corporate Governance identify universal tenets for countries seeking to devise or retain an effective corporate governance framework, including the rights, roles and responsibilities of stakeholders, shareholders and the governing board of companies. In terms of monitoring and implementing its Acts, the OECD has no power or authority independent of its members. Instead the OECD polices legal instruments through a mixture of "deliberation, persuasion, surveillance and self-regulation."[44] Provisions for peer review are an integral part of some OECD instruments such as the Codes of Liberalization of Capital Movements and Current Invisible Operations. Likewise, parties to the OECD anti-bribery agreement commit to "cooperate in carrying out a programme of systematic follow-up to monitor and promote the full implementation of this Convention."[45] The OECD appraises most ordinances, however, through ongoing surveillance or as part of more generalized peer reviews like the *Economic Survey*.

States negotiate legal agreements at the OECD for three principal reasons. First, legal governance at the OECD represents a halfway house giving additional moral force to the informal knowledge-based consensus but without states indulging in the kinds of formal commitments that would follow from the negotiation of a fully fledged international treaty in another forum. Second, they can deal with issues disproportionately affecting OECD countries, especially in areas where divergences between OECD and non-OECD members would obstruct a formal treaty in an international institution with a wider membership. Noticeably, almost a third of OECD Acts concern the environment, where the "contentiousness and potential grandstanding"[46] in more universalist institutions such as the United Nations Environment Programme (UNEP) have made international agreements notoriously difficult to reach. Third, OECD agreements are flexible. The exposition of loose guidelines rather than prescriptive frameworks permits legitimate differences between national approaches, preventing one prickly issue from derailing an entire covenant. Many OECD Acts permit participants to nominate exemptions when they sign up (although subsequently they can only reduce these exemptions rather than add too them), and contain general standards that "allows states to adapt their commitments to their particular situations rather than trying to accommodate divergent national circumstances within a single text."[47]

Averaging less than five legal agreements per year, the OECD is hardly a riotous legislator. Nevertheless, as befits the organization's expansive remit, OECD legal governance pierces an array of economic sectors, prompting one respected commentator to designate the OECD amongst a triumvirate, alongside the WTO and the IMF, of international economic institutions "that provide a framework of rules for the world economy."[48] OECD agreements may be esoteric but their effects are all around us. In 23 countries, the OECD Scheme for the Application of International Standards for Fruit and Vegetables determines whether the fruit and vegetables that supermarkets import and you purchase are designated Class I or Class II. Indeed without these international quality standards these comestibles may never have been available in the first place because importers could not be sure of what they were procuring. The OECD Scheme for Seed Certification ensures that farmers producing these crops can obtain seeds whose quality is guaranteed and which is appropriate for their land. The container trucks you pass every day on the freeway will, if they are transporting volatile chemical substances, sport labels conforming to classification criteria agreed at the OECD.

OECD legal governance is also rolled out through other institutions. A series of the OECD's environmental recommendations have been partially or wholly incorporated into the agreements or procedures of other bodies. For example, the Food and Agriculture Organization's 1985 International Code of Conduct on the Distribution and Use of Pesticides superimposed the notification system at the heart of the OECD's 1984 Recommendation on Information Exchange Related to Export of Banned or Severely Restricted Chemicals.[49] Sometimes, as

Chapter 1 noted with regard to the World Bank's and FSF's use of the organization's corporate governance principles, OECD frameworks are monitored as part of the procedures of other bodies. Private institutions also laud OECD agreements. For example, in 2001 the International Network of Pensions Regulators and Supervisors endorsed the OECD's Fifteen Principles for Regulation of Occupational Pensions.[50]

The balance of opinion seems to be that OECD legal governance has allowed international cooperation to progress further than it otherwise would in a variety of areas, in particular the liberalization of trade and investment and the management of environmental problems. That said, the OECD's "soft" approach to legal governance possesses similar drawbacks to the normative dimension of OECD governance. Lacking an exact set of commitments or a formally prescribed punitive framework for transgressors limits the OECD's capacity to generate "international incentives for national policymaking" and allows states to pay lip service to the agreements they have signed.

The Anti-Bribery Convention exemplifies the experience. Only the churlish would deny the achievements following the signing of the convention in 1997. Participating states have passed legislation to outlaw bribery of overseas officials anywhere in the world, with tough penalties for those convicted; created dedicated units to investigate and prosecute these laws; and improved aisles for exchanging information. In an interview on the 10th anniversary of the convention, Mark Pieth, chair of the OECD Working Group on Bribery, claimed 30 individuals or corporations had been punished for infractions of laws passed under the rubric of the convention and another 150 investigations were in train. Moreover, the convention is motivating corporations to develop rigorous internal procedures to deter the use of backhanders to secure business overseas.[51] Nevertheless, serious shortcomings persist. Signatories have the legal frameworks but are less assiduous in harnessing them. Transparency International claims there is "little or no enforcement"[52] of the convention in 18 of the 37 participating states, only 11 countries have brought "major cases" under their legislation, and eight have not brought any cases.[53] Angel Gurria concedes that "rather than being more ambitious, some countries are sliding back on their determination"[54] to tackle bribery. His view gained further credence in December 2006 when the U.K. government shelved the investigation into alleged bribery in Saudi Arabia by British Aerospace Systems Limited, arguing that national security concerns trumped its commitment to the convention. This contravenes Article 5 of the convention, which states that in matters of enforcement parties "shall not be influenced by considerations of national economic interest, [or] the potential effect upon relations with another State."[55] Given the latent competitive advantages accruing to national economies offering sweeteners to malfeasant officials, actions like the U.K.'s could weaken the resolve of those tenaciously pursuing corruption and help to unravel the agreement.

Palliative governance

The previous section demonstrated that compared with commensurate international organizations the OECD does not engage to any great degree in the production of international law and, where it does, is deprived of formal powers to secure compliance. Nevertheless, "an international organization may be important not for what it 'does' in legalistic terms, but for what it helps other organizations do and for what it helps its own members accomplish outside."[56] This, the sum of the many ways the OECD's hidden hands massage the wider processes of global governance, is the palliative dimension of OECD governance.

The OECD's functions have always overlapped with other international organizations. However, as Henry Aubrey's 1967 analysis of the organization argued, this "should not lead inevitably to the verdict of redundance. On the contrary, what the OECD can do in preparation for, or collaboration with, other bodies is precisely the question that needs investigation."[57] Unpretentious activity in the OECD has throughout been critical to the ongoing circus of international summitry and efforts to conclude treaties in related international institutions. Nicholas Bayne, the U.K.'s permanent representative to the OECD from 1985–88, fittingly christened the OECD as the "Cinderella amongst international organizations ... it does not always go to the balls like its grander sister organizations, though it often runs up their dresses and sometimes clears up the mess after the party."[58]

This support comes in several guises. First, the OECD compensates for scarcities in resources and expertise afflicting other bodies. In trade, for example, "the OECD's research and investigatory capacities have been important ... because of the GATT/WTO's limited budget for these activities."[59] Despite a growing membership and the complexity of trade issues being adjudicated, GATT's secretariat never numbered over 400.[60] The WTO, a body with an even larger membership and remit, has a meager 630 officials. Consequently many WTO activities such as the Trade Policy Reviews, the periodic peer reviews of the trade policies of specific members, habitually draw upon the OECD secretariat's reports and statistics.[61] Other institutions, most notably the "gaggle of G's"[62] (the G8, G8 ministerial bodies, G20 and so on), have no permanent secretariat and, as Chapters 1 and 5 document, their deliberations have come to rely heavily on the OECD's data, ideas, and analytical work. Second, the organization acts as a pre-negotiating forum for leading players in the international system. Before states can engage in meaningful negotiations in formal decision-making contexts, let alone reach a final accord, the issue needs to be clarified to a point where states are able to determine their national interest. In other words, there must be some baseline "consensual knowledge" about key terms, the nature and causes of the problem, and how the costs and benefits of different solutions will be apportioned amongst negotiating parties. Cohn's analysis of the organization's pre-negotiation of trade issues prior to their emergence in the GATT/WTO suggests that pre-negotiation at the OECD has three discrete stages: elucidating the parameters of the issue and hypothesizing about how to address it; investigation of these hypotheses by the OECD secretariat in preparation for more meticulous dialogue and analysis; and seeking consensus among OECD members to carry forward into formal negotiations elsewhere.[63]

Chapter 1 demonstrated how the OECD's prenegotiation of government procurement, services, and agricultural trade expedited their inclusion in the GATT. GATT principles to prevent environmental standards being used as a protectionist measure derived in major part from the OECD's work on national treatment and non-discrimination. Staying with the environment, the OECD in the 1980s ratified several acts pertaining to the shipment of hazardous waste from OECD countries. These principles and guidelines went on to form the nucleus of the UNEP negotiations leading to the 1989 Basel Convention on the Control of Transboundary Movements of Hazardous Wastes and their Disposal.[64] Similarly, the "polluter pays" principle contained in the OECD's 1972 Recommendation on Guiding Principles concerning International Economic Aspects of Environmental Policies, which states that polluters bear the costs of controlling and preventing environmental contamination, underlay the declarations reached at the 1972 UN Conference on the Human Environment and the UN "Earth Summit" in Rio in 1992. The final stage, where the OECD acts as a caucusing group in other bodies, can be controversial because it gives the impression of its (mainly) developed members ganging-up on developing countries. Furthermore, as the number of systemically important economies lying outside the OECD grows, the OECD's utility as a mechanism for resolving disputes between *all* the relevant players diminishes (see Chapter 5).

Third, the OECD is a post-negotiating and implementation forum. Despite the OECD's best efforts to finesse the issues, negotiations in formal setting frequently stall or descend into outright rancor. On these occasions, the OECD offers a private and undemonstrative ambiance where unofficial talks can continue. For example, following heated exchanges prior to and during the 1982 Versailles summit, G7 leaders thought they had a joint commitment on trade with the communist bloc and, in particular, the export credits they could offer. The consensus abruptly dissolved with the French and German governments insisting the agreement had no material implications for their policies toward trade with countries behind the Iron Curtain. The perception that they were backtracking on their commitments led the United States to extend an embargo on the supply of energy equipment and technology to the communist bloc to include subsidiaries and licensees of American companies abroad. The Europeans reacted angrily, accusing the United States of reneging on the commitments made at Versailles, prompting the *Financial Times* to infer that "the components of the Western Alliance are coming apart."[65] That conflict over East–West economic relations did not cause terminal damage to the Western alliance was down to the less politically fraught environment of the OECD, where the issue "was quietly resolved"[66] over the next year.

Other topics enter the OECD not because they have reached a dead-end elsewhere but owing to exasperation at their sluggish progress or because countries feel their grievances may receive a more sympathetic hearing in the OECD. One of the reasons tax competition emerged as an issue in the OECD was because the EU's attempts to conclude an agreement became mired in ideological discord, clashing national interests and, most problematically given the rights of states to veto the EU's fiscal directives, an unwillingness to surrender sovereignty. Despite the controversy over the initiative, the OECD was able to conclude a series of recommendations to counter tax competition, spurring parallel action in the EU. Once countries autograph international agreements the OECD sometimes plays a role in monitoring and implementation. The OECD's techniques for assessing and differentiating greenhouse gas emissions underscore the work of the Intergovernmental Panel on Climate Change and the implementation of the UN Framework Convention on Climate Change (UNFCCC).[67] Pressure evoked through the OECD's surveillance and peer review processes also encourages states to work toward pledges made in other forums. G8 countries know, for instance, that DAC peer reviews and annual reports will cast a critical eye over their performance in regard to the aid commitments appearing in summit communiqués.

On top of furthering the work of its sister organizations, the OECD's other palliative role is as "an ideal partner to fill some of the gaps in addressing global challenges."[68] There are no hard and fast rules about why states devolve issues to the OECD. Nevertheless, the nature of the OECD gives it a comparative advantage in mulling over certain kinds of topics. A great strength of the OECD is an aptitude for pondering interdisciplinary problems. Most international organizations have tightly prescribed competences and, moreover, the way their "secretariats are organized does nothing to compensate for the divisions and the rigidities that are inherent in all government structures but, rather, tends to intensify them by setting up parallel structures."[69] In contrast, the OECD's remit is broad and its directorates are willing to unite to tackle complex interdisciplinary problems.

In the early 1990s, countries were casting around for an organization to investigate the effects of higher labor standards on trade and investment flows and whether they detrimentally affected economic competitiveness. Furthermore, if labor laws did damage competitiveness, they wanted to know if states with higher labor standards should apply protectionist measures to goods imported from those with anemic labor standards to avert "a race to the bottom," i.e. countries could use trade barriers to retain competitiveness rather than filleting their labor standards. The need for an organization with expertise in trade, investment, and labor market policies left the OECD as "the ideal partner" to fill the void. The collaboration of the directorates of Employment, Labor and Social Affairs (ELS), DAFFA, and Trade resulted in a landmark 1996 report, *Trade, Employment and Labor Standards: A Study of Core Workers' Rights and Labor Standards*. The report found that high labor standards had a negligible impact on economic competitiveness or trade and investment flows. Furthermore, there was no necessary correlation between trade liberalization and levels of worker rights. The "report both confirmed the consensus support of OECD Member countries for core labor rights and laid the groundwork for the ILO Declaration on Fundamental Principles and Rights at Work."[70]

The labor standards case study pinpoints another beneficial spin-off from interdisciplinary work at the OECD, namely that it forces officials from separate domestic ministries to collaborate. Sharing the report's authorship between three directorates fused bureaucrats from the trade and labor ministries of participant states into single national delegations. Consequently,

> officials who most likely did not communicate with one another in their own capitals were forced to forge common national

positions. ... [and] the publication process required separate ministries within national governments to consider seriously the linkages between labor rights and trade, competitiveness, and foreign direct investment.[71]

Correspondingly, the OECD's Environment Directorate has cohabited with those responsible for agriculture, taxation, development, energy, and trade. Contributors to this "joint work invariably agree that the experience in OECD forums makes a positive difference in their working relationships with colleagues from other ministries and agencies back in their capitals."[72] A second favorable side-effect of the OECD's interdisciplinary exertions is a capacity to perceive the interlinkages between policy domains. Indeed "there are subjects which exist largely because OECD detected a connection between apparently unrelated themes: trade and investment; development aid and the environment; tax collection and money laundering."[73] In short, the OECD's ability to deal with topics that are "functionally divided" elsewhere confers the organization with a "unique capability for the joint consideration of related policy issues."[74]

A second set of topics where the OECD has a comparative advantage in plugging gaps in global governance are those exclusively or disproportionately involving OECD member states, especially if the organization has acknowledged expertise in this or a related area. Traditionally, the OECD has made a sensible venue to locate specific concerns because its membership includes most or all states with a serious stake in the issue. The rationale for locating discussions of excess capacity in the aluminum and steel industries in the OECD in the 1970s was that the OEEC and OECD had monitored the industry since the 1940s and OECD members accounted for 70 percent of aluminum production and consumption.[75] By pitching participants into a discursive rather than a decision-making environment, states have possibly been more flexible in their approach, allowing greater progress to be made in the OECD than in a formal negotiating context. Equally, the floating of the ill-fated MAI initiative at the OECD partly reflected antagonism to such a deal from developing countries which would have led to logjam at the WTO, but also that OECD countries sourced 85 percent of FDI outflows and hosted 60 percent of FDI inflows[76] and that the OECD's Codes of Liberalization were the nearest thing to a comprehensive legal agreement to govern FDI.

Lastly, the OECD plays a "system-tending" role "spotting new problems and problems that have long lead-times, and of stimulating work on them before they become critical or unmanageable."[77] The most visible manifestation of this is the OECD's International Futures Programme hatched in 1990. Today's policymakers inhabit a world of bewildering complexity, making it exceedingly difficult to plan for the long-term future. Making full use of the OECD's protracted experience of tackling complex, interdisciplinary problems, the International Futures Programme

> helps decision makers meet this challenge via improved monitoring of the long-term economic and social horizon; more accurate pinpointing of major developments and possible trend breaks; greater analytical appreciation of key long-term issues; and better dialogue and information-sharing to help set policy agendas and map strategy.[78]

Since the initial projects on the rise of China, air transport, infrastructure policy, and capital markets, the Futures Programme continues to thrive and is today tracking the long-term outlook for the management of food, energy, technology, infrastructure, money, risk, natural disasters, terrorism, and outer space.

Conclusion

At a symposium marking the OECD's thirtieth anniversary Sylvia Ostry, head of the Department of Economics and Statistics from 1979 to 1983, pronounced that "a great advantage of the OECD is that it has no power but great influence."[79] While the OECD has no troops to deploy and does not lend money with menaces, the notion that the organization has influence is prima facie verification that it does wield some power in global governance. Furthermore, states hardly clamor to bankroll otiose institutions, suggesting the OECD does, in modern parlance, "add value" to our ability to manage our common affairs. The OECD spurns the limelight but invisibility does not mean impotence. Throughout the Cold War the OECD and its members upheld capitalism and democracy as the mainstays of global governance. The triumph and continued success of the "OECD world" bolstered these values as the finest foundations for global governance and something to which others should aspire. Because it is the largest international economic organization predicated exclusively on capitalist and democratic principles, belonging to the OECD is a badge of honor bestowed on states that embrace and seek to export values offering the optimum route to peace and prosperity.

The "ongoing process of organized cooperation"[80] in OECD bodies, including data production, information exchange, conceptual innovation, policy analysis, and policy learning through surveillance and peer review sounds prosaic. These consultations do not lead to overnight resolutions but over a long period of time the values, ideas, and principles agreed at the OECD become norms which percolate the national and international policymaking circuitry. Occasionally, the members take their consensus one stage further, enacting formal legal agreements whose strictures signatories are duty-bound to implement. Lastly, without the OECD the wider processes of global governance would hurriedly atrophy. As well as being a dustbin for awkward international issues, the normative and legal consensus developed at the OECD regularly becomes the basis for formal treaties negotiated in other global institutions. The OECD has an enviable record of developing, or helping other institutions to develop, ideas, norms and rules to govern a medley of economic and social issues. The next chapter looks in detail at some of the pressing issues presently under the OECD microscope.

4   Current issues

To convey a flavor of the OECD's sprawling undertakings and its contribution to global governance, this chapter sketches some of the paramount issues under discussion in the organization. The chapter commences with areas overtly mentioned in the OECD Convention such as sustainable economic growth, trade, and development before looking at some of their tacit outgrowths including taxation and private sector governance. Later sections examine a host of environmental, technological, and social matters that are now more prominent in the OECD's portfolio. Where appropriate the derivation of present work is teased out, especially if the OECD's interference exerted an invasive influence on present-day thinking or practice. The main focus, however, is upon topical OECD interventions in the form of ideas, publications, datasets, and peer reviews (normative governance), OECD Acts (legal governance), and collaborations with other international institutions (palliative governance).

Sustainable economic growth

Sustainable economic growth is the OECD's central preoccupation and the objective to which most other sectors detailed in this chapter are ultimately aimed. The ECO is by far the largest and most powerful OECD directorate, keeping a firm grip on the organization's tiller. Along with its two main committees the EPC and EDRC, the ECO is the department that swallows the biggest slice of the OECD's resources and sets the dominant economic paradigm within which the remainder of the organization's program of work resides. The ECO strives to understand the interface of macro- and structural economic issues and the interdependence between the policies of individual countries. Consequently, few recesses of the OECD are uncontaminated by its influence. Led by the ECO, the prescriptions of many OECD directorates are inundated by recommendations to unleash or extend the cleansing and invigorating gale of market forces. Governments and the world's financial press eagerly await the OECD's economic policy evaluations. Accompanying the 20 or so *Economic Surveys* released each year by the EDRC (see Chapter 2) are the OECD's other flagship economic productions, the bi-annual *Economic Outlook* and the annual *Going for Growth*. Published under the auspices of the Secretary-General, the *Economic Outlook* prophesies about economic trends for the two years ahead and commends policies for governments to sustain global economic growth. It contains a "general assessment of the macroeconomic situation" in the OECD, chapters featuring economic developments in each member state and, since 2005, chapters about Brazil, India, China, and the Russian Federation. As well as a sizable statistical annex, the *Economic Outlook* has synopses of the ECO's empirical work on matters of a contemporary comportment. Prescient recent examples include policies to cope with rocketing oil prices and the "credit crunch" (June 2008), the perils of ascending household debt (December 2006), gauging underlying inflation (June 2005), the U.S. current account deficit (June 2004) and the aftermath of the telecommunications bubble (June 2003). Publication of the *Economic Outlook* began in 1967 but *Going for Growth* is a modern vintage. Inaugurated in 2005, it gazes explicitly on structural policy developments in OECD countries and their role in determining differential rates of economic growth. The report enunciates a range of internationally comparative indicators and thematic studies of selected structural policies, stressing best practices, and quantifying progress toward the recommendations of the preceding report.

The ECO studies many structural policies in conjunction with other departments and directorates. There are, however, two multidisciplinary initiatives involving the ECO that warrant separate attention. The Political Economy of Reform project recognizes that while the distress from structural policy changes is sometimes instant and perturbs defined sections of society, the benefits are often dispersed and materialize afterwards. Therefore while recommending growth-enhancing reform is straightforward, even courageous and domestically secure politicians may flinch or be derailed by those agitating for the status quo. The ECO's work on the Political Economy of Reform provides hard evidence of the rewards from structural policy change that governments can "sell" to overcome opposition and build coalitions for reform. The second initiative is the Innovation Strategy. At the 2007 MCM, ministers noted that "innovation performance is a crucial determinant of competitiveness, productivity and national progress, and that it is an important key to addressing global challenges such as climate change and sustainable development."[1] Equally, they perceived considerable variations in government policies, the dexterity of national innovation systems, and the need to reflect upon the emergence of cross-national systems of innovation transpiring from the globalization of production and commerce. They commissioned the OECD to exploit its fortes in entrepreneurship, regulation, the economics of health, education, and sustainable development to chisel out a compendium of best practices to stimulate innovation.

Trade and agriculture

The Doha Development Round is the latest deal to benefit from the OECD's efforts to strengthen the rules-based multilateral trading system and maintain the momentum of trade liberalization. The OECD is "upstream"[2] of the Doha process. Outside the WTO, the OECD persuades states to participate in the negotiations by allaying misconceptions about free trade and providing, beside the World Bank and the United Nations Conference on Trade and Development (UNCTAD), capacity building measures to ensure the effective participation of developing countries. Inside the WTO, it supplies internationally acclaimed information and analysis to defuse conflicts and lubricate the negotiations.

The prickliest problem, which caused the most recent talks to collapse in July 2008, is agriculture. The OECD estimates that its members dispensed $258 billion in agricultural support in 2007, 23 percent of OECD farm producers' gross receipts.[3] Agriculture is arguably the most erudite dimension of the OECD's trade work. The mastermind of the analytical tools and models that solved agricultural contradictions in the Uruguay Round and curator of the world's most catholic data on agricultural exporters, the OECD is uniquely positioned to undertake comparative research and extend its application to developing countries. Signaling this, and a prospective desire to improve efficiency, the OECD merged its trade and agriculture directorates in 2006.

The Trade and Agriculture Directorate's (TAD's) spotlight falls on trade-related effects of domestic agricultural support. These policies are reviewed annually and the results printed in *Agricultural Policies in OECD Countries: Monitoring and Evaluation* one year and the abridged *Agricultural Policies in OECD Countries: At a Glance* in the next. OECD reviews of non-member agricultural policies erupted in the 1990s in the former communist regimes of Eastern Europe, but of late have grown in importance. For the first time in 2005, the OECD undertook dedicated reviews of agricultural policies in Brazil, China, and South Africa. Subsequently, the OECD launched the biennial *Agricultural Policies in Non-OECD Countries: Monitoring and Evaluation* in 2007. Using an identical approach to that directed at OECD countries, this report winnows the agricultural policies of Brazil, Bulgaria, China, India, Romania, Russia, South Africa, and Ukraine. The protectionist sentiments accompanying food price inflation look set to assure the salience of the OECD's agricultural work for the foreseeable future.

OECD reconnaissance and norm building persists in support of the WTO and UNCTAD's management of trade in services and to advance discussions related to government procurement, customs policy, trade and investment, and trade and competition, the so-called Singapore issues. Export credits, however, are one area where legal governance takes precedence. The Arrangement on Officially Supported Export Credits marked its thirtieth anniversary in 2008 and the OECD continues to widen the scope of the agreement. The latest version refreshes the ordinances of the sector understanding on export credits for ships and introduces a new sector understanding on export credits for civil aircraft. This latter development is significant, as Brazil became the first non-OECD country to join part of the agreement. This is symptomatic of the surge in export credits from non-members, a key challenge now facing the OECD's export credit regime. Strides have also been taken to link export credits to other aspects of OECD work. The OECD passed a recommendation to deter bribery in export credits in 2006 and revised the recommendation concerned with the environmental impact of projects benefitting from export credits in 2007.

Development

Sustainable worldwide development is part of the OECD's raison d'être. The 23 members of the DAC, the hub of development issues at the OECD, disbursed $104.4 billion in ODA in 2006, over nine-tenths of the global total.[4] DAC's subsidiary bodies reveal the enormity of the OECD's development agenda. Nine working parties and networks deal with development statistics, aid effectiveness, gender equality, development evaluation, the environment, poverty reduction, governance, conflict, peace and development cooperation, and fragile states. In addition to those from member and non-member governments, representatives from international organizations and major non-governmental organization (NGO) networks participate in these consortia. These include the IMF, the International Labour Organization (ILO), the World Bank, regional development banks, and more than a dozen UN agencies. NGO networks, primarily from the environmental field, incorporate the World Conservation Union and the International Institute for Environment and Development.

Together with the 90 staff of the Development Co-operation Directorate (DCD), the DAC's chief purpose is to assist member states to accomplish pledges made in accord with the MDGs. Data reported by DAC members is collated into internationally consistent digests of ODA flows and policies, most notably the *International Development Statistics* and the annual publications the *Development Cooperation Report* and *Development Aid at a Glance*. A renowned leader in this field, the OECD has evolved tools such as the Creditor Reporting System that disaggregates ODA figures to highlight the destination and ambitions of individual development projects. The DCD is also the secretariat for the Partnership in Statistics for Development in the 21st Century (PARIS21). Instigated in response to a United Nations Educational, Scientific and Cultural Organization (UNESCO) resolution, PARIS21 nurtures discourse between statisticians from across the globe to improve the quality of development data, thereby enhancing the prospects for enlightened policymaking. At the moment, PARIS21 is persuading poorer countries to unfurl plans capable of producing "nationally owned and produced data for all MDG indicators by 2010."[5]

DAC also founds peak practices for ODA and a context where countries make commitments to advance them. DAC has released 28 guidelines, recommendations, and reference manuals since 2006.[6] Occasionally these standards, such as the landmark 2001 DAC Recommendation on Untying Official Development Assistance to the Least Developed Countries, are elevated to the status of OECD Acts. In 2005, DAC members said they would increase ODA by $50billion to $130billion by 2010 (doubling aid to Africa as part of the package) and wheedled officials from 60 countries and organizations to sign the Paris Declaration on Aid Effectiveness. The declaration identifies 12 indicators to measure progress in development partnerships and reform ODA delivery. Lastly, four-yearly peer reviews of DAC members monitor the volume and cogency of ODA, their adherence to DAC best practices, and their own national and international aid pledges.

Critics excoriate the DAC as docile and illegitimate, maintaining the "D" is the poor relation in the OECD. To placate concerns about legitimacy, the DAC and wider OECD Development Cluster are expanding dialogue with non-members and civil society. Formed in 2006, the Global Forum on Development's inaugural task is to pinpoint policies to improve the effectiveness of development finance.[7] The seventh edition of the *African Economic Outlook*, published jointly with the African Development Bank in 2008, encompasses the experiences of 35 countries and the OECD now has an Africa Desk to unify and extend work in the region.[8] Concurrently, the debut of the *Latin American Economic Outlook* in 2007 denotes the further extension of the organization's fingers into South America. Scratching the ineffectiveness itch is more troublesome. DAC's figures parade OECD donors falling pitifully short of the promises made in 2005 and the UN target for developed countries to devote 0.7 percent of their GNI to ODA. The average DAC member donated 0.46 percent of their GNI to ODA in 2006. This figure plunges to 0.31 percent for DAC countries taken collectively because the large absolute ODA offerings by bigger DAC members like the United States and Japan masks the miserly percentage of their GNI.[9] Critics also question whether the DAC's starting premise that countries are responsible for their own development is compatible with its and the wider OECD's fondness for neo-liberal solutions that expose developing countries to the vicissitudes of international capitalism.

Taxation

Consumption taxes, international tax dispute resolution, environmental taxes, harmful tax practices, tax administration, transfer pricing, and the effects of taxes on economic activity form the nucleus of the themes trawled by the CTPA. The common element knitting the OECD's tax agenda together is the inverse relationship between the ease with which factors of production cross national borders and the nuisances posed to national revenue authorities responsible for levying taxes upon them. Empirical evidence supporting wilder claims about this inhibiting international transactions or prompting a "race to the bottom" in national tax rules is thin.[10] Nevertheless, the disjuncture between national tax raising powers and the global economy plus the heightened interdependence of national tax regimes induces states to fumble for common approaches or even outright cooperation at the OECD.

The most hallowed OECD tax edict is the Model Tax Convention. Postwar reintegration swelled the numbers of economic entities operating in multiple jurisdictions. This aggravated the irritant of double taxation, where revenue authorities in two or more jurisdictions simultaneously impose levies on the same economic activity. Bilateral conventions confined double taxation through exemptions and allowances for taxes forfeited overseas. However, in the absence of a universally accredited model on which to erect bilateral treaties, a miasma of deals based on disparate definitions, rules, and principles materialized. Their susceptibility to alternative interpretations was costly for enterprises and a godsend for tax dodgers.[11] The OEEC Fiscal Committee busied itself with the problem and in 1958 published the first installment of what, in 1977, became the Model Tax Convention on Income and on Capital. Throughout the 1980s, the OECD Committee on Fiscal Affairs (CFA) deliberated over revamping the convention in response to economic liberalization. Realizing this was a continuous enterprise, the CFA adopted an ambulatory Model Convention in 1991 to permit speedier renewal without dictating a total overhaul. In recent times clauses on the taxation of income from cross-border pension issues, shipping and air transport, tax treatment of employee stock options, software distribution, and the definition of royalties have been added to the convention. The convention is one of the OECD's most influential pieces of legal governance. More than 3,000 bilateral tax treaties, many involving one or more non-OECD country, follow the customs of the convention.

The convention touches upon two other prominent fiscal ventures at the OECD, transfer pricing and tax avoidance and evasion. Transfer pricing refers to the values allocated to goods, services, and assets traded within a corporation. The corporation rather than market forces set these rates. Accordingly, corporations can reduce their tax burdens by setting prices in ways that apportion profits to subsidiaries registered in lenient tax jurisdictions. The explosion of multinational corporations inflamed the issue and forced transfer pricing's inclusion in the Model Tax Convention. Article 9 of the convention maps the "arm's length principle," stating that transfer prices ought to equate roughly to those haggled by independent firms in the market place. The 1979 Recommendation on the Determination of Transfer Pricing between Associated Enterprises exhaustively elucidates formulae to apply the arm's length principle. The OECD updated the guidelines in 1995 and perseveres in the vanguard of international rules and norms for transfer pricing.

At times, the transfer pricing rules appear utopian. They assume that multinational corporations willingly cooperate with tax authorities and that tax authorities willingly cooperate with each other. In actuality, treasuries hemorrhage billions in tax revenue because corporations and rich individuals secrete assets in jurisdictions where stringent confidentiality laws forbid sharing information with tax collectors overseas. The OECD's Harmful Tax Competition initiative intended to stop to this by prohibiting certain tax practices and committing states to greater transparency and information exchange. Shorn of its more intimidating clauses (see Chapter 1), the initiative has yet to achieve its objectives. Nevertheless, the OECD is orchestrating a quiet revolution on tax secrecy. Thanks to the peer pressure aroused at the Global Forum on Harmful Tax Practices, 45 of the 47 harmful tax regimes identified in OECD countries were eradicated or found not to be harmful.[12] By moderating its bellicose rhetoric, the OECD persuaded 35 non-member jurisdictions to give oaths to improve transparency and information exchange. The jurisdictions once disparagingly dubbed "harmful tax havens" are now "participating partners" in the OECD Global Forum on Harmful Tax Practices. Their incorporation has supplemented the legitimacy of the initiative and isolated as pariahs those few places (Liechtenstein, Andorra, and Monaco) still rebuffing it. A budding consensus amongst the 80 or so countries attached to the global forum is yielding concrete rules clarifying tax information exchange. Building upon Article 27 of the 1977 Convention, the 2002 Model Agreement on Exchange of Information in Tax Matters expounds principles to underscore information exchange. Since 2007, 16 bilateral Tax Information Exchange Agreements based on these standards have entered into force, bringing the total number to 27.[13] Switzerland and Luxembourg's incorrigible opposition notwithstanding, the initiative is inching forward and may eventually reach a "tipping point" where even devout opponents will succumb to widely consecrated norms.

Private sector governance

Today, partly thanks to the liberalizing policies pursued by members in the OECD, capital flows largely unmolested across the frontiers of OECD countries and market actors infect the everyday life of their citizens to an unprecedented degree. The jumping incidence and magnitude of financial crises require regulations to ensure market signals transmit incentives for private actors to fight market abuse, and *manage* risks as well as take them. Given the bulk of production and investment activities are within and between OECD countries, the DAF is a suitable venue for these undertakings.

The anti-bribery convention (see Chapters 1 and 3) is simply one aspect of the OECD's multifaceted assault on corporate malfeasance. The bosses of the world's preeminent competition bureaus assemble in the Competition Committee, which "promotes market-oriented reform by actively encouraging and assisting decision-makers in government to tackle anti-competitive practices."[14] The committee's priorities comprise trimming regulatory impediments to competition, mergers and anti-trust principles, and curtailing the manipulative behavior of monopolies and cartels. Legal governance in the form of recommendations on hard-core cartels (1998), regulated industries (2001), and mergers (2005) plus a host of informal best practice guidelines fronts the committee's work but, as with the other aspects of OECD legal governance, this depends on the prior existence of a normative consensus. Here the analytical sway of the secretariat, in particular the Competition Division of the DAF and the cornucopia of seminars, workshops, and conferences they organize and the networks they engender, are essential. The formation of the Global Forum on Competition in 2001, marshaling the representatives of over 70 competition authorities from around the world, ensures that OECD best practices increasingly resonate globally. Nevertheless, scholars are hesitant about the effects of the OECD on national competition policies. While admitting that OECD definitions of anti-competitive practices are acquiring widespread currency and that more thorough reporting is broadening collective knowledge, this has not manifested itself in glittering reforms in national capitals.[15]

Insurance, pensions, and investment are three other areas where members are entreating the OECD to act. The Insurance and Private Pensions Committee liaises with the international financial institutions and international networks such as the International Association of Insurance Supervisors (IAIS) to identify policies to manage risk. So decisive is insurance to economic activity that it has merited a permanent place on the OECD agenda. In 1963, the then Insurance Committee's study, *The Control of Private Insurance in Europe*, pioneered the international comparison of insurance regulation and supervision in European countries and underpinned three decades of cooperation and liberalization at the OECD.

The concerns surrounding the liberalization and regulation of insurance markets persist, and are now coupled with mastering risks arising from terrorism and environmental cataclysm and the "pension crises" looming in OECD countries. Ageing populations and shortfalls in public and private pensions schemes threaten to impoverish pensioners and saddle governments with responsibility for financing the welfare of retirees. OECD research is grasping for ways to ensure that private pensions can compensate for the declining munificence of public provision and that consumers make educated purchases of financial products. To this end, the Global Pensions Statistics Project initiated in 2002 fashions indicators to judge the resilience of national retirement systems. The OECD Council has sanctioned 11 insurance and pensions related recommendations since 2002, making it the fastest expanding precinct of OECD legal governance. These include the Core Principles of Occupational Pension Regulation (2004) and the Guidelines on Funding and Benefit Security in Occupational Pension Plans (2007), the solitary international standards governing occupation pensions. In 2008, two years after a mandate bestowed by the G7 finance ministers, OECD work on financial education came to fulfillment. Two recommendations identifying good practices to improve financial literacy with regard to pensions and insurance were accompanied by the International Gateway for Financial Education, a website for experts to share their ideas and experiences.[16]

Agreed in 1961, the OECD Code of Liberalization of Capital Movements and the Code of Liberalization of Current Invisible Operations enshrined progressive liberalization, non-discrimination and transparency as principles to guide the elimination of curbs upon international capital flows and services trade. The codes steadily expanded to reflect financial interdependence and the sophistication of financial instruments. The OECD appended futures, swaps, and options to the Capital Movements Code in 1992 and, a decade subsequently, overseas investments by pension funds and insurance companies.[17] Now the OECD is examining the applicability of the codes' principles to state-owned investment vehicles, so-called sovereign wealth funds (SWFs). SWFs have existed since the 1950s, but their newfound size and location outside the OECD have given rise to apprehension about their implications for financial stability and national security. Petitioned by the G7 finance ministers and in juxtaposition with the IMF, the OECD is cultivating guidelines that are consistent with the code's craving for openness yet allow recipient countries to protect their security.

Environment

If the OECD were to rewrite its convention, environmental aspirations would probably appear explicitly amongst the organization's aims. Since bursting onto the scene in 1970, environmental matters have become interwoven with the OECD's work on economic growth, trade, energy, investment and multinational enterprises, agriculture, and development.[18] Economic considerations again lurk behind the OECD's curiosity in this topic, with the organization viewing a well-fettled environment as "a pre-requisite for a strong and healthy economy."[19] Environmental enactments are the most populous arena of OECD legal governance but it is for its normative and palliative roles that the OECD's Environment Directorate (ENV) and its cast of supporting bodies are commemorated. The ENV provides "policy advice based on reliable environmental data, outlooks and cross-country experiences,"[20] enabling governments to ameliorate their environmental performance and facilitating the activities of international organizations such as the World Bank, WTO, UNEP, WHO, and the UNFCCC.

Much of the organization's contemporary environmental program derives from the *OECD Environmental Strategy for the First Decade of the 21st Century*, adopted by OECD environment ministers in 2001.[21] Progress on the strategy is patchy. Underpinned by the principles existing in mechanisms of OECD legal governance and international agreements such as the Kyoto Protocol, the strategy outlines impressive targets for managing the climate, freshwater, and biodiversity, and decoupling environmental degradation from economic growth in energy, transport, and agriculture. The principal surveillance mechanisms, the Environmental Performance Reviews and individual chapters in the *Economic Surveys*, betray the failings of OECD countries to comply with these targets. More optimistically, recent OECD reports examining the costs and distributional consequences of environmental policies provide governments with evidence to defrock those arguing that demanding environmental rules impair economic growth and burden the poor.[22]

Seven years after the Environmental Strategy, the sequel, the *OECD Environmental Outlook to 2030* appeared to bolster the case. Unlike its predecessor, the report incorporates large non-member countries and highlights the availability and affordability of policies and technologies to confront environmental challenges. It restates that the long-term benefits of implementing these policies and technologies outweighs the short-term costs, and paints a bleak picture of the penalties of procrastination, especially on "red light" issues where only immediate action will shirk environmental catastrophe.[23] Sizable media coverage forced the governments of several OECD countries to defend their record, but whether this translates into policy changes remains to be seen.

Greater success befell the project's efforts to augment environmental indicators and international cooperation. Based on its gilded reputation in the field, the OECD continues to harmonize environmental indicators internationally and is the custodian of reputable datasets and accompanying analysis. Predicated on the OECD's widely touted "Pressure-State-Response" model, the OECD Core Set of environmental indicators assist with adjudicating progress toward environmental targets. Meanwhile the periodically produced *Environmental Data Compendium* depicts key environmental trends in OECD countries. These mountains of environmental data are also condensed into the annual OECD *Key Environmental Indicators*.[24] OECD figures are used extensively in environmental policy debates in member countries. In terms of international cooperation, the OECD's Global Forum on Sustainable Development founded in 2002 brings specialists from member and non-member countries together to exchange ideas and decipher policies connected with environmental aspects of sustainable development. Successive MCM communiqués have made plain the significance of OECD environmental analysis to recent and forthcoming events, including G8 summits and the proceedings of the UN Climate Change conferences.[25]

A second notable ingredient of OECD environmental work is that pertaining to the Environment, Health and Safety program and chemical safety and biotechnology in particular. Designed to inhibit distortions in the trade of chemical products and tighten rules to shield the environment and human health, its role in chemical safety "can be legitimately cited as one of the OECD's most outstanding environmental successes."[26] Over 120 OECD Guidelines for Testing of Chemicals are in operation[27] and chemical control accounts for almost an eighth of OECD legal governance. Though they are esoteric, several OECD standards and guidelines are venerated as global best practice, not least the 1981 Decision of the Council concerning the Mutual Acceptance of Data in the Assessment of Chemicals, known by the acronym "MAD." Signatories to MAD agree to accept the validity of chemical safety data produced in counterparty countries, providing that its production conforms to the rules of the Guidelines for Testing and the OECD's Principles of Good Laboratory Practice. The corollary is that the generation of data happens only once because after the scientific authorities in one country declare a chemical safe other signatories will trust their verdict. By obviating repeat trials, MAD saves governments and businesses €60 million a year[28] and discourages the use of chemical safety as a non-tariff barrier to trade.

In 1980, the STI commenced investigation into biotechnologies and their potential application. The rapid commercialization and soaring trade in biotechnologies, plus public anguish about the effects of genetically modified organisms, have since pushed biotechnology onto OECD health, agriculture, and environmental agendas. The OECD's most prominent recent achievements are in the province of genetics and genomes. For example, the use of genetic testing by medical practitioners to forecast or diagnose disease dates to the early 1980s. Increasingly, however, genetic testing is an international service necessitating the transfer of genetic data between states espousing radically different regulatory frameworks. The 2007 Recommendation on Quality Assurance in Molecular Genetic Testing weaves together these varying approaches and identifies internationally agreed best practices in this area. The Recommendation on the Licensing of Genetic Inventions, and the Recommendation Concerning Access to Research Data from Public Funding, both promulgated in 2006, aim to help countries promote research and innovation within the bounds of commercial and public acceptability. The former concedes that patents are indispensible props to innovation but sets guidelines to ensure that exploiting this research does not prejudice access to medical commodities and services. The latter inclines governments to disclose the fruits of research developed using public monies.

Science and technology

The STI's virtues are not restricted to the world's laboratories. The directorate's analytical insights also assist governments to devise policies that harness science and technology to further economic and social wellbeing. Typically, rigorous performance indicators fortify the analysis and recommendations. Published in alternate years, the *OECD Science, Technology and Industry Scoreboard* and the *OECD Science Technology and Industry Outlook* excavate over 200 internationally comparable indicators to narrate trends in national innovation strategies and isolate policies that contribute to industrial competitiveness. The biennial *Information Technology Outlook* and the *OECD Communications Outlook* recite similar functions but focus specifically on ICT.

The advent of the knowledge economy and the weight attributed to microeconomic drivers of economic growth has given science and technology a special resonance. The OECD is increasingly engrossed in detecting the supreme blend of policies to unlock the potential of ICT. The Committee on Consumer Policy, and the Committee for Information, Computer and Communications Policy (ICCP), for example, delve into issues surrounding the information infrastructure, e-commerce, information security, and regulation. Even as most obsess with weapons of mass destruction others worry that the addiction of prevailing economies and societies to ICT leaves them vulnerable to "weapons of mass disruption,"[29] meticulously planned attacks by hackers and terrorists, that maim critical parts of the ICT infrastructure. The OECD continues to investigate the roles and responsibilities for governments, industry, and individuals in preventing malicious strikes.

Matters of information security and e-commerce are intimately intertwined. Trembles over the security of online transactions, especially those undertaken abroad, still daunt e-commerce. The OECD's Guidelines on the Protection of Privacy and Transborder Flows of

Personal Data (1980 and updated in 2003) predated most national legislation in this area. In 1999 and 2003, the OECD passed recommendations designed to protect consumers, and the organization is presently concentrating on the problem of "phishing" and related aspects of cyberfraud. The Committee on Industry, Innovation and Entrepreneurship (CIIE) complements this by examining how ICT, human capital and entrepreneurship intersect at firm and industry-wide levels. Partly, this is concerned with *systems* of science and innovation and ensuring technology moves from the drawing board to the productive process. Equally, the CIIE ponders the skill upgrades and organizational changes obligated by ICT and its impact on global industrial restructuring.

The OECD is contributing to the governance of specific industry sectors. The uppermost are shipbuilding (with a dedicated committee dating to 1966) and steel (with a dedicated committee dating to 1978), industries disfigured by protectionism and subsidies. The Working Party on Shipbuilding and the Steel Committee bring together countries representing 95 percent and 60 percent of production respectively to discuss the problems blighting the industry in a non-negotiating context.[30] Discussions in these bodies are improving the transparency of the industries, but agreements on the utmost issues are proving elusive or impossible to implement.

Energy

Erratic oil prices and anxieties about climate change and energy security have thrust the IEA and the Nuclear Energy Agency (NEA), two of the OECD's semi-autonomous agencies, back into the limelight. The IEA festoons its 27 members with data and policy advice on energy security, economic development, and environmental protection, the professed "Three E's" of energy policymaking.[31] The IEA Energy Statistics Division supervises the assembly and dissemination of vast amounts of information about global energy markets, especially oil. The monthly *Oil Market Report* surveys interim movements in global oil markets and prognosticates about the coming year. Complementing this are the five-year forecasts of the twice-annual *Medium Term Oil Market Report* and the protracted projections for energy markets in the *World Energy Outlook*, the IEA's stellar testimony. Based on its analysis of energy trends, the *World Energy Outlook* gives policymakers ideas about how to navigate between seemingly paradoxical goals such as meeting the escalating demand for energy consumption whilst cutting greenhouse gas emissions in line with international agreements.

These data are also the raw materials for policy-oriented IEA studies. Recent commentaries have appraised the security of oil supplies, improving energy efficiency in fossil fuel power generation, surmounting barriers to energy-efficient investments, and pathways to more sustainable technology policies. Brief surveys of energy policy developments in IEA members occur annually, and formal peer reviews take place in four-year cycles. Both harvest insights about successful energy policies.

In 2005, the G8 leaders invited work from the IEA on 13 separate matters as part of the Gleneagles Plan of Action on Climate Change, Clean Energy and Sustainable Development.[32] The G8 stamp stimulated the IEA to evolve roadmaps for 17 technologies needed to halve energy-related CO_2 emissions by 2050, develop internationally comparable measures of energy efficiency, make 25 proposals for energy efficiency improvements, commence dialogue with major non-IEA members, and deepen dialogue with the private sector.[33] The 2008 G8 Summit asked the IEA to refine indicators to compare energy efficiency across industry sectors, continue its mapping exercise, especially on carbon capture and storage and advanced energy technologies, and vowed to implement the IEA's 25 energy efficiency recommendations.[34]

With countries casting round for inexpensive, low emission alternatives to fossil fuels and memories of the devastating accidents at Three Mile Island and Chernobyl receding, nuclear power is poised to emerge from the doldrums. The mothballing of nuclear reactors in many NEA members has depleted knowledge about the economic, scientific, and technical after-effects of nuclear power amongst government officials. The NEA, celebrating its 50th anniversary in 2008, is ready to fill the breach. Founded by the OEEC as the European Nuclear Energy Agency (the European prefix was dropped in 1972 to reflect membership of non-European states) the NEA exists to promote the safe, economical, and environmentally friendly use of nuclear energy. The NEA's 28 members account for 85 percent of global nuclear power capacity. Each year around 500 experts collaborate in the NEA's technical committees on safety and regulation, radiological protection, radioactive waste management, nuclear law, and nuclear science. Every year the NEA produces over 60 reports and policy papers containing agreed positions on controversial subjects such as recycling nuclear waste and preventing fissile materials from reaching terrorists and rogue states.[35]

Employment and labor

As approbated by the convention, the OECD promotes policies to maximize sustainable levels of employment. The ELS monitors trends and policy initiatives in national and international labor markets and considers their relationship with broader social and economic policies.

Vocational education, easing migration and integrating migrant personnel, encouraging previously marginalized groups (the disabled, juvenile and older workers, and those with domestic ties) to enter the labor market, and countering opposition to traumatic but crucial reforms were at the heart of the pathfinding OECD studies of the 1960s[36] and reverberate in the ELS' contemporary agenda. What is different, reflecting the tenor of the times, is the diagnosis which places the duty to become an employable and self-reliant member of society squarely upon the individual. Nowhere is this better illustrated than in the follow-up to the OECD Jobs Strategy.

When employment and labor ministers convened at the OECD in 2003, the climate of high and persistent unemployment that incubated the jobs strategy had subsided. Undeterred by studies skeptical of the extent to which this transformation was down to following its prescriptions,[37] ministers solicited a retrospective on the jobs strategy to assess the efficacy of earlier recommendations and their pertinence for fledgling challenges. These challenges entailed reducing obstacles to labor market participation to milk the talents of the 35 percent of people of working age in the OECD without employment, and devising policies to ensure not only more jobs but also superior jobs justifying higher salaries.[38] This would alleviate a conundrum plaguing welfare states in OECD countries, namely how to finance a growing army of pensioners with a shrinking workforce. Finally, the integration of emerging economies and their plentiful labor could mean momentous dislocations for OECD countries with rigid labor markets or menial workforces.

The 2006 *OECD Employment Outlook*, the OECD's annual anthology of employment trends and policies, presented the reassessed jobs strategy. Generally, the reassessed strategy reiterates and extends the recommendations of its predecessor and buttresses the organization's employment-related pursuits. The strategy reminds governments that long-term employment prospects depend first, on a stable macroeconomic framework, and second, measures to boost human capital to allow their inhabitants to thrive in a globalized economy (see the section on education below). A third prong, labeled "active labor market" policies, is reform to tax and welfare systems to coax people to join, stay in, or return to the workforce. Three volumes resulting from the "Sickness, Disability and Work Project"[39] explore the impact of sickness and disability benefits in 12 countries. Meanwhile surveys of eight of the 16 countries involved in the OECD "Jobs for Youth Project"[40] made suggestions to burnish the transition from full-time education to full-time employment. In 2006, the OECD distilled the lessons from 21 country reviews of ageing and employment policies into the report *Live Longer, Work Longer*. This urged assistance to help older workers remain employable, financial incentives to stay in the workforce and postpone retirement, and overhauling employment practices to encourage hirers to recruit, retrain, and retain older staff.[41] Lastly, the strategy again lauds regulation and deregulation to amplify labor market flexibility.

Migration too is a longtime OECD affair given fresh impetus by the 2001 MCM's call to "deepen and extend its analysis of the economic and social impacts of migration in both host and origin countries, including the international mobility of workers at different skill levels."[42] A key focus, gauged in depth since 2002 by the *Economic Surveys*, is the economic upshot of migration. Theoretically, migration is a positive sum game whereby receiving countries overcome skills scarcities and originator countries accrue remittances and, when they return home, individuals that are more proficient. Nonetheless, in practice, migration is tricky for receiving and originator countries. The OECD's recent statement *Jobs for Immigrants* (2007) is the initial episode of the organization's work considering the host government's role in surmounting the language, skill, and qualification hurdles that hamper the assimilation of migrant workers.[43] Likewise, the "brain drain" caused by qualified employees departing to fill vacancies in OECD countries may dowse development elsewhere. In conjunction with the WHO, the health and migration divisions of the secretariat are monitoring the correspondence between health and migration policies and streams of health care personnel with a view to articulating recommendations to protect the health care systems of OECD and non-OECD countries alike. The OECD announced the preliminary findings in the 2007 *International Migration Outlook*, the yearly keynote appraisal of migration trends, data and policies.

Education

Despite being feted as "a kind of 'eminence grise' of the education policy of industrialized countries,"[44] education only attained prominence within the OECD during the 1990s.[45] The principle of "lifelong learning for all" endorsed by OECD education ministers in 1996,[46] the launch of PISA in 1997, the creation of a dedicated Directorate for Education (EDU) in 2002 and the Global Forum on Education in 2005 puts the OECD on a par with, or some argue overtakes,[47] UNESCO as the premier supplier of educational statistics and sculptor of education policy agendas worldwide. That said, several education-related projects, amongst them PISA and the Centre for Educational Research and Innovation (CERI) created in 1968 to glimpse long-term education scenarios, depend on Part II budget contributions, implying that education is not yet deemed a core OECD activity.

The EDU's mission is "to assist members and partners in achieving high quality lifelong learning for all, contributing to personal development, sustainable economic growth and social cohesion."[48] Of this triumvirate, EDU's overarching concern is securing economic competitiveness. EDU applies normative governance, especially the development of internationally comparable indicators and timely policy analysis, to usher governments toward strategies to improve educational outcomes. Of the OECD's educational initiatives, PISA continues to cause the biggest splash, with national media outlets and opposition parties in many participating countries, Germany being a notable example, seizing on poor performance in PISA to demand improvements to education systems. Based on standardized tests and questionnaires, PISA is the only international survey dedicated to measuring the reading, mathematical, and scientific literacy of those about to leave compulsory schooling. The triennial survey allows states to plot their progress toward educational targets, to compare best practices and learn from the experiences of their peers. Andreas Schleicher, the head of the education directorate's Indicators and Analysis Division, suggests the most useful function of the PISA survey is to demonstrate what can be achieved, stating "in 1995, at the first meeting of OECD ministers I attended, every country boasted of its own success and its own brilliant reforms. Now international comparisons make it clear who is failing. There is no place to hide."[49] The scale (and hence the potential influence) of PISA grows with each survey cycle. Whereas 43 countries, mainly OECD members, participated in the inaugural 2000 PISA survey, 67, now with OECD members in the minority, are enrolled for the 2009 assessment.[50]

Jointly with UNESCO and Eurostat, the OECD compiles and hosts a database of educational statistics submitted by national governments and its keynote annual publication, *Education at a Glance*, summarizes and analyzes the latest statistics. Importantly, however, this document and the various policy and thematic reviews disseminated by the EDU go further than the sheaf of competing organizations because they employ statistics not just to "compare characteristics of national education systems but also to compare underlying political decisions."[51] In other words, the OECD is unmistakably concerned with *how* government policies shape the education sector and identifying the *best* strategies for enhancing education systems. There are several other strings to the organization's lifelong learning bow. Complementing PISA's focus on teenagers are programs on childhood education and care policy and higher and adult education. The 2006 report, *Starting Strong II*, gleaned the lessons of OECD research on pre-school education and care policy.[52] The report highlighted how government investment can eradicate disparities in provision and improve the long-term public budgetary situation by bolstering childhood development. Australia's Labor government is amongst those invoking the report in support of its reforms to early childhood services.[53] The OECD's Program on Institutional Management in Higher Education handles university education. This program examines the relevance of the nature and extent of higher education funding to the knowledge economy. It also encompasses dilemmas surfacing from the internationalization of education systems, in particular the difficulties baffling aspiring students from assessing the quality of higher education programs in different countries. The OECD worked with UNESCO to formulate the Guidelines for Quality Provision in Cross-Border Higher Education ratified by Council in 2005, one of only three pieces of OECD legal governance in the education field. Also under the adult education remit is the Programme for the International Assessment of Adult Competencies (PIAAC). Modeled on PISA, PIAAC will evaluate and compare the extent to which adults have the skills required to flourish in the knowledge economy and identify policies to plug deficiencies. The inaugural PIAAC survey will take place in 2011.

Health

In some respects, the OECD's record in the health care sector mirrors that of education. First, the OECD was for many years an esteemed purveyor of cross-national health data but it was not until the turn of the millennium and the embarkation of the OECD Health Project that it infiltrated the mainstream of the organization's work. In 2004, the first ever OECD health ministers meeting concluded the project and acted as a fillip for further work. A year later the OECD created a separate health division of the secretariat within the ELS directorate and a health group which transmuted into the OECD Health Committee in 2007.

Second, the OECD achieves influence through normative furrows, prioritizing the development of statistical tools to equate the performance of health care systems and inform policy debates. For example, the System of National Health Accounts, co-authored with the WHO and Eurostat, is an internationally agreed framework for pooling and reporting health care expenditures. Similarly, the OECD leads the Health Quality Indicators Project, which is a network of experts from the OECD, WHO, European Commission, professional organizations, and academics that conquers methodological problems to comparing national health systems and elaborates international indicators to measure technical differences in health care quality such as survival rates, waiting times for treatment, and aspects of patient safety.[54] Currently the project is refining systems on patient safety, inventing ways to enable international comparisons of the responsiveness of health care systems and levels of patient satisfaction, and attempting to conceive the first internationally compatible database for mental health care. The OECD is a prolific publisher of health statistics. Each year it releases the *OECD Health Data* containing 1,200 indicators of the robustness of health care systems in OECD countries. The 2008 edition for the first time incorporated figures for the numbers of foreign trained doctors, the incidence of vaccine-preventable diseases, and care for the elderly.[55] The biennial publication *Health at a Glance* browses trends in, and the divergent quality of, health care in OECD countries. Despite this and some well received reports concerning long-term elderly care and the ramifications of private health insurance, the OECD is foremost a statistical guru rather than the supreme shaper of national health care policies.[56]

A third resemblance between the OECD's health and education portfolios is their motivation by economic imperatives. By raising rates of economic activity and productivity, an efficient and effective health care system can contribute enormously to a nation's economic vibrancy. In 2005, OECD countries spent an average of 8.9 percent of their GDP on health care, with three-quarters of the resources financed from the public purse.[57] With ageing populations and medical advances exacerbating the upward pressure on health care expenditure, the OECD's work under the rubric of the Economics of Health is spearheading efforts to identify policies to reconcile spiraling costs with providing the health services required for economic and social wellbeing. Interestingly, however, ECO rather than ELS is the home directorate for this venture, raising suspicions about the downgrading of social facets of health care at the OECD in favor of recommendations to advance economic efficiency. Recent *Economic Surveys* of the United Kingdom, Portugal, Canada, Norway, Hungary, Sweden, Luxembourg, Germany, Iceland, Denmark, Russia, and Chile have all contained chapters on health care, exhibiting the growing salience assigned to this area in the OECD as a structural determinant of economic vitality.

Conclusion

This overview of current OECD activities raises or re-emphasizes several points. The OECD is, first and foremost, an economic organization. The smorgasbord of subjects studied by the OECD is ultimately united by a desire to understand the relationships between different domains in order to promote policies to deliver sustainable economic growth. Second, non-members splice virtually all areas of the OECD's work. Third, the normative aspect of OECD governance prevails over the legal aspect. The staple focus is gathering, processing and disseminating data, fleshing out issues, elaborating lines of action in the light of national experiences, and monitoring their implementation through surveillance and peer review. This is not to deny the importance of the OECD Acts in force but to acknowledge that the organization normally stops short of solidifying the consensus attained into legal governance. Fourth, the palliative dimension of OECD governance is undiminished. Mostly the OECD operates unobtrusively by sieving data and surfing policy debates. Nonetheless, this nondescript activity means that when a crisis hits or the priorities of clients change, the OECD is the "go to" institution for policymakers, politicians and the media because it is, or is perceived to have the nimbleness to become, the leading repository of information and expertise for the problems in vogue. The next chapter ponders whether the OECD's reform program is sufficient to repulse the phalanx of other institutions hovering to play this role.

5 OECD reform

In 2003 Jorma Julin, then Finnish ambassador to the OECD, penned an article containing a fictitious advertisement for a vacancy in the global governance architecture:

> Wanted: International organization to help governments manage the following global challenges: sluggish growth; unemployment; health care; ageing; trade protection; development; poverty; corporate malpractice; tax evasion; global warming; assessing future risks, and more. Commitment to fostering sustainable development and higher living standards in all countries is required. Experience and expertise essential. Must have a strong membership and excellent references.[1]

He gave an honest appraisal of how an imaginary selection panel would receive a prospective OECD application for this position, one extraordinarily similar to the organization's own. They would marvel at the OECD's knack of colonizing and roving across the declared issue areas, delineating the relationships between them, and identifying policies for governments to fulfill their domestic and global objectives. The relatively large secretariat, a pool of experts with almost 50 years of accumulated knowhow, and the committee system, which uniquely immerses national bureaucrats and is where peer pressure is exercised, would also count in the OECD's favor. Conversely, the panel would vacillate over deficiencies in OECD membership and some lukewarm testimonials. Would an organization that excludes China, India, Russia, Indonesia, Brazil, and other emerging industrial giants be a legitimate or effective arbiter of global challenges? Why do some referees admire alternative venues such as the EU, G8 or G20? Would it make more sense to entrust some or all of these subjects to more specialized government networks such as the

FSF, private think tanks, or hybrid institutions like the World Economic Forum? Julin concluded that although it might make the shortlist, only a reformed OECD could be confident of successfully applying for this post. Providentially, as Chapter 1 described, the organization's hierarchy agreed and embarked under Donald Johnston upon a renewal agenda including membership enlargement and outreach to non-members and civil society. Couched in the agenda were proposals to fix the four dimensions of OECD governance. In terms of cognitive governance, the scheduled changes, especially the recruitment of additional members with a commitment to "fundamental concepts like market-based economy and democratic principles,"[2] would reaffirm capitalism and democracy as principles ingrained within the OECD community, trumpet the triumph of these values in a growing number of states, and bolster them as norms to which others should aspire. The proposals would enhance normative governance by incorporating more countries within the OECD's statistical reporting systems, giving the secretariat a more complete picture on which to base their analysis. The fresh perspectives brought by both state and non-state actors would reinvigorate the committee system, enriching peer learning and the development of the consensual knowledge upon which the OECD trades. Adjunct voices would augment not only the quality but also the legitimacy and applicability of OECD ideas and the various acts of legal governance erected upon them. The confluence of these benefits would finally secure the OECD's palliative role. With a strengthened identity, more relevant and legitimate ideas, plus extensive global linkages through which to diffuse them, the OECD would become once again the default setting for debate, analysis and forging common ground amongst the world's leading states, and regain its influence in other international bodies.

This remainder of this chapter contemplates the achievements and present status of the reform program and its capacity to realize the anticipated benefits. The next two sections adumbrate the OECD's present and projected programs with reference to enlargement and outreach to non-members, and outreach to civil society. The third section examines prospects for the consummation of the OECD–G8 nexus, especially in the aftermath of the 2007 G8 summit's decision to use the OECD as the podium for the Heiligendamm Process, the G8's own non-member outreach strategy. The chapter traces the tensions within and between the components of the reform package. The OECD must carefully manage these tensions if it is to disarm its opponents without debilitating the organization by drastically altering its personality.

OECD enlargement and "enhanced engagement"

Since his appointment as Secretary-General, Angel Gurria has repeatedly said the OECD needs to act as a "hub of globalization"[3] with the aptitude to shape the economic policies of the twenty-first century. The catch, as Donald Johnston, the outgoing Secretary-General, put it is "how are you going to shape the global economy if you're basically working with a minority of it?"[4] The roots of today's economic imbalances often stem from the actions of the "Big Six" non-OECD members. When it comes to managing balance of payments strife for example, the G20 is a more sensible choice than the OECD's WP3. As well as providing the same private forum for frank discussion of the subject, the G20 welcomes China and Russia, possessors of the world's first and third most abundant foreign exchange reserves. Similarly, it seems preposterous to suggest the OECD's syndicate of environmental bodies can figure out solutions to the world's climate and energy problems without China, India, and Brazil. Enticing new members and enhancing the role of non-members within the OECD are thus vital ingredients in reforming the organization.

The 2007 MCM invited "the Secretary-General to set out the terms, conditions and process for the accession"[5] of Chile, Estonia, Israel, the Russian Federation, and Slovenia. The Council adopted accession roadmaps for these countries in November 2007[6] and in January and February 2008, Deputy Secretary-General Thelma Askey headed "kick-off" missions with ministers and senior officials in the candidate countries. Excepting the Russian Federation, which envisions a longer process, these countries are hopeful of becoming OECD members in 2010.[7] These accessions will enhance cognitive governance by widening the pool of market democracies. However, it is difficult to aver that these accessions will revolutionize the other dimensions of OECD governance. These countries might be "likeminded" enough for OECD membership but, again excepting the Russian Federation, the world's sixth biggest national economy by GDP,[8] they are hardly the "significant players" referred to in the Noburu Report (see Chapter 1) that will pacify those taking aim at the legitimacy of the OECD's normative and legal governance or the obsolescence of its palliative governance. Chile (the 43rd biggest economy) and Israel (52nd) are middle-ranking economic powers, but Slovenia (77th) and Estonia (98th) are minnows. To put this in perspective, on the World Bank's rankings of countries by GDP Slovenia is sandwiched between Guatemala and the Yemen, while Estonia nestles between Uganda and Jordan.[9] Benefits for normative governance may also be limited because the Russian Federation,

Chile, Israel, and Slovenia are currently the four non-members most embroiled in OECD committees. The five accession states hold over 40 percent of non-country observerships in OECD committees (see Table 2.5). To banish these criticisms the signs are that the OECD's enlargement strategy is set to become more aggressive. Including the five accession states, the OECD claims 16 countries "have expressed interest"[10] in membership. Six European states (Bulgaria, Cyprus, Latvia, Lithuania, Malta, and Romania) and South Africa have officially indicated that they wish to join. China, India, Brazil, and Indonesia are, albeit more ambivalently, on this list and the OECD views membership for these countries as a possible outcome of its enhanced engagement program (see below).[11] Furthermore, the OECD is giving "priority ... to South East Asia with a view to identifying countries for possible membership,"[12] none of whom appears in the above roll-call. Should the OECD comprise these 16 countries and a smattering of Southeast Asian states it would mollify those who denigrate the organization as elitist and illegitimate. Nevertheless, their accessions are fraught with practical and political problems.

From a practical standpoint, this inclusivity and legitimacy could come at the cost of incapacity and sclerosis. This number of members may overload the committee system. Even with 30 members, certain OECD committees, such as the lynchpin EDRC, are already at bursting point.[13] A further influx would mean attenuating the frequency, quality, or scope of peer reviews with negative implications for normative governance. Moreover, new members could abrogate the gains derived from streamlining of the committee system. First, they may covet OECD investigations of areas of particular interest to them, further fraying the organization's PWB. Second, they would protract the secretariat's task of gathering and analyzing information and the search for consensus in committee, rekindling the debate about the timeliness of OECD advice and undermining the organization's palliative governance. The quest for consensus is likely to be particularly irksome. Achieving consensus amongst 30 likeminded members is exasperating enough, but with the diversity of countries on the OECD's list of potential members, it could prove hopeless. The changing quarters for OECD meetings are a salutary metaphor. OECD committees used to meet in bijou rooms in the Chateau de la Muette with participants seated around a conference table. Now they mainly convene in the cavernous chambers of the OECD's conference center where, sitting in a horseshoe configuration, the physical void between the participants sometimes symbolizes the ideational chasms between them.[14] Another allegory that the OECD may heed is the experience of the Organization for Security and Cooperation in Europe (OSCE), another consensus-based institution, "crippled"[15] by clashes between pro-Western and pro-Russian states.

Financing is the final practical issue confronting a dynamic membership expansion. The OECD's work program is heavily reliant on voluntary contributions, which have soared from just 6.3 percent of the organization's budget in 1995–96 to 30 percent in 2007–8.[16] The resource-intensive nature of the OECD's surveillance means the accession of every extra member adds 1 percent to its expenditure,[17] running the risk of reviving the bickering over funding that beleaguered the organization in the 1990s.[18]

All of these glitches are soluble, but engender further problems of their own. Allowing countries to opt out of chosen committees and legal Acts (as the present governance structure mandates) or extending QMV could avert tortuous consensus building processes, but shunning core committees or Acts would ignite a debate about the value of these countries to the OECD. Extending QMV requires a unanimous council decision. Assuming the OECD could overcome quibbles about voting shares and the majority needed to carry a motion, it is unthinkable that the smaller countries would relinquish their equal voting rights with the larger powers on a wholesale basis. Another possibility is the greater use of sub-groups, working parties and committee bureaus to consider specific aspects of an issue. Committee bureaus, for instance, normally comprise the committee chair and vice-chair, and three to six national delegates to steer, alongside the secretariat, the committee's work. Nevertheless, the OECD would still have the delicate challenge of deciding the basis on which to compose the bodies.[19]

To cope with potential funding issues, the OECD agreed that applicants would bear the costs of accession and is phasing in a decade-long financing package announced at the 2008 MCM.[20] The OECD is plugging funding gaps with voluntary contributions for specific projects. This might be a boon for the OECD, hyping its deftness and guaranteeing that benefactors are interested in the results. The danger is that this will sponsor a hand-to-mouth approach that weakens the OECD's normative governance by undermining its talent for spotting, and thinking about ways to handle, farsighted issues such as climate change and fossil fuel depletion and "create inappropriate incentives for those whose jobs depend on such contributions."[21] Moreover, funding shortages exacerbate the handicap of bigger powers skewing the OECD agenda by using voluntary funding to subsidize "friendly" initiatives whilst stifling others by withholding it.

An enlargement program encompassing these 16 countries could also run aground on a lack of political will on the part of the Big Six and internal dissension within the OECD ranks. Possibly as part of a strategy to inveigle them into their dominant rules-based system and thereby hamstring their freedom of action, the OECD's G8 members are keen that the Big Six non-member economies, especially China and India, eventually join the OECD. Unhappily, China and India demonstrate little enthusiasm for OECD membership. Both are wary of cozying up to the OECD lest it detrimentally affects their nascent South–South relationships or that it would indeed impose intolerable restrictions on their ability to exercise their newfound power.[22] Of the others, the Russian Federation and South Africa are the most whole-hearted pursuers of OECD membership, Brazil somersaults, while Indonesia's Minister for the Economy has stated the country has "yet to consider joining as an option."[23]

Internal disagreements are problematic for the OECD, as all existing members can veto accessions. Historical animosities pose some specific snags. Turkey, for instance, might veto Cypriot accession. More general problems surround precisely who will join and in what sequence. Japan and Australia are pushing for a larger Asian caucus, the EU believes its new members should head the queue, and, as previously mentioned, the larger OECD members make the case for the big non-member economies. Smaller members quiver about this final point. The exclusive membership and soft power approach gives them more clout in the OECD than in the more universal international institutions, something that the incursion of gigantic members would diminish. This might be preferable, however, to retaining power in an unreformed and less influential OECD.

At present, OECD membership for the Big Six is a faraway prospect. A steadfast refusal to eliminate capital controls, endemic bribery and corruption, politically manipulated statistics, and inferior bureaucratic arrangements are just some of the reasons why these states would not pass muster with the gauntlet of technical assessments by OECD committees. Moreover, although the convention is silent on the matter and authoritarian regimes once resided in the OECD, it is nevertheless the case that political "matters (for example on democracy, rule of law, human rights etc.) may be considered as particularly important parameters for judging whether a candidate country ultimately should be invited to join OECD."[24] None of the Big Six can realistically claim to uphold democracy, the rule of law, and human rights.

The dilemma then for the OECD is that while the current batch of accession countries are likeminded but not significant players, the significant players are insufficiently likeminded. Their accession would be blocked by existing members or would dilute and damage the identity of the OECD community. The OECD's solution, as part of the multi-tiered global relations strategy described in Chapter 1, is the "enhanced engagement" program. This program is for non-members which are unwilling or ill equipped to assume the rigors of accession but without whose participation the OECD could not deliver its global mandate. As the title of the program implies, what differentiates the program from previous OECD interactions with non-members is the intensity and extent of their participation. Although the OECD will tailor programs for individual countries, each will entail a mix of "Committee participation, Economic Surveys, adherence to instruments, integration into the statistical reporting and information systems, sector specific peer reviews and other policy dialogue initiatives."[25]

With the Russian Federation undergoing the accession process, the envisaged participants in enhanced engagement programs are Brazil, China, India, Indonesia, and South Africa. The hope is that repeated exposure to normative governance through full participation in information exchange, policy dialogue, and peer reviews, the OECD's values and ideas will percolate and take root in these countries and stimulate the reforms necessary to make them eligible for OECD membership. The OECD acknowledges that this will be a protracted process but that in the interregnum it could assist the palliative dimension of OECD governance. The regular and widespread participation of these sizable non-members in OECD bodies will leaven their attractiveness as places where the world's systemically important economies can thrash out their problems, a factor which may have motivated the G8's decision to use the OECD as a platform for the Heiligendamm Process (see below). The drawback is that because these countries are nonchalant about OECD membership, the OECD is unlikely to elicit sweeping changes in their behavior.

Outreach to civil society[26]

In the 1990s, intellectuals, politicians, and bureaucrats rediscovered the concept of civil society. Scholars endlessly contest the traits and functions of civil society,[27] but for the purposes of this section it is defined as the dominion where an armada of non-governmental actors strives to calibrate the rules governing social life.[28] Mainstream understandings of global governance proceed from the premise that states and state-centric international organizations are the main propellers of the world's economic agenda and relegate non-state actors to the perimeter. Some scholars scold this "top-down" mentality and point to the power of civil society organizations (CSOs) that, separately of states and international organizations, can energize global governance from the bottom-up.[29] O'Brien et al. argue that since 1980 the engagement between CSOs and multilateral economic organizations has stimulated a "transformation in the nature of global economic governance"[30] classed as "complex multilateralism."[31] Complex multilateralism connotes a situation where states are still the chief arbiters in international organizations but are interspersed with a greater number of more assertive civil society actors. The input of BIAC and TUAC notwithstanding, until the 1990s much of the OECD conformed to the "top-down" model of global governance. Largely detached from civil society, state actors essentially mediated the OECD's agenda. To some extent, this reflected the OECD Council's restrictive interpretation of Article 12 of the Convention permitting the organization to maintain relations with non-member entities. A 1962 council pronouncement affirmed:

> Any international non-governmental organization may be consulted by the Organization provided that it satisfies the following three conditions:
> (a) it has wide responsibilities in general economic matters or in a specific economic sector;
> (b) it has affiliated bodies belonging to all or most of the Member countries in the Organization; and
> (c) it substantially represents the non-governmental interests in the field or sector in question.[32]

Few groups in the then hatchling global civil society met any of the council's provisos, and those with the wherewithal to target international organizations tended to converge on those with ample operational assets such as the UN. The maturation of global civil society expanded quantitatively those CSOs eligible for consultation with the OECD. Nevertheless, it was the MAI imbroglio (see Chapter 1) that finally brought home to both parties the myopia of ignoring the other. The MAI exploded any illusion CSOs held that the OECD was an arcane think-tank unrelated to their constituents' interests. CSOs became conscious of the power of the OECD's communities of influence to sway agendas in national capitals and those international organizations with operational competences. Moreover, because OECD discussions occur before national positions ossify, dialogue with the organization provides a better opportunity for influence than in international organizations steeped in formal bargaining and negotiation. For its part, the

OECD thought new interfaces with civil society would yield fresh perspectives, a tonic to pep up normative governance. It was felt that incorporating the ideas of a heterogeneous audience and possibly engrossing CSOs in shadowing activities could neutralize those lambasting the illegitimacy of OECD legal governance. Supportive cliques could also counter misconceptions about OECD prescriptions.

After the clarion call in the 1990s, the OECD's posture toward consorting with civil society altered under the three interrelated headings of communication, dialogue, and participation.[33] The MAI fiasco lay bare the clogging of the OECD's arteries for communicating with civil society by bureaucrats or brigades agitating for the status quo. Predominantly the anti-MAI crusade was orchestrated online. Activists uploaded a blizzard of websites. These sites were sometimes erroneous; nonetheless, they were incendiary and comprehensible. Contrastingly, the OECD dithered for over a year before uploading a pro-MAI website indecipherable to all but technical experts. In 1997, the OECD unified responsibility for its external image and liaisons into a new Public Affairs and Communications Directorate (PAC). The PAC filters OECD communications to pare back the possibility of conflicting messages emanating from different directorates. The PAC pays additional attention to what the OECD communicates and customizes it for specific audiences. The website, face-lifted to ease navigation, is now the chief OECD communications intermediary, receiving over 15 million visitors in 2006.[34] Over 4,700 institutions subscribe to *SourceOECD*,[35] the "OECD's online library of statistical databases, books and periodicals,"[36] and in December 2007 the organization introduced OECD.Stat. Using a single query in OECD.Stat, researchers can forage for information across a multitude of OECD databases and drop them into a personalized spreadsheet. *CivSoc*, the OECD civil society newsletter published regularly since 2005, is also available online.

If communication infers the spreading of the OECD's message to civil society, "dialogue" signifies a two-way relationship where CSOs can put their point across, in or to, the organization. In 2006, the OECD consulted over 200 NGOs on more than 100 topics.[37] Most dialogue occurs via OECD committees, which are free to attune their relationship with civil society as described in Chapter 2. The CIME has gone farthest in taking civil society to its bosom. Ahead of revising the Declaration on International Investment and Multinational Enterprises in 2000, the CIME embarked upon the OECD's "first truly public consultation process."[38] By strengthening the bonds amongst CSOs trying to promote corporate accountability and sustainable investment, the process reared a new alliance, OECD Watch. OECD Watch has 79 members from 41 countries,[39] including 31 members from 19 non-OECD members. The coalition's members are committed to:

> Monitoring and contributing to the work of the OECD's Investment Committee;
> Testing the effectiveness of the OECD Guidelines for Multinational Enterprises as a corporate accountability tool;
> Disseminating information to civil society groups, particularly in developing countries, about the work of the Investment Committee, corporate governance and the OECD Guidelines; and
> Advising and supporting NGOs about filing complaints against companies alleged to have breached the OECD Guidelines.[40]

In 2004, the CIME and CMIT merged to become the Investement Commitee. As well as liaising with the Investment Committee after each plenary session, designates of OECD Watch sit on Investement Committee Roundtables on Corporate Responsibility and the annual meetings of the National Contact Points whose job it is to champion adherence to the Declaration at the domestic level.

Consumer policy is another field recently infested by civil society. Consumers International is a full participant in a clutch of OECD working parties and seminars, and lent a hand in 2005 to the drafting of guidelines to protect consumers from international swindlers. Concomitantly, Public Voice, a flotilla of organizations dedicated to confidentiality and consumer interests, contributed to the drafting of OECD Guidelines for Cryptography Policy (1997) and the 2002 revision of practices to secure information systems and networks.[41] OECD bodies concerned with the environment and agriculture have longer standing arrangements with civil society. A battalion of 7,000 experts from industry, academia, trade unions, and environmental CSOs convenes in working groups of the Environment Directorate to renew and police the Good Laboratory Practices related to the OECD's 1981 Mutual Acceptance of Data (see Chapter 4).[42] The OECD Committee for Agriculture's consultations with civil society stretch back to 1962, since when the International Federation of Agricultural Producers and the European Confederation of Agriculture have "participated regularly"[43] in its work.

A fuzzy line divides dialogue and participation, with the latter signifying the formalization or institutionalization of the relationships between civil society and the OECD. In some cases, for example, CSOs play their part in the monitoring the implementation of OECD legal governance. A prominent illustration is the contribution of BIAC,

TUAC, Transparency International and the International Chamber of Commerce to the peer review mechanism of the OECD's anti-bribery convention. The Working Group on Bribery oversees this peer review process. CSOs do not participate in the evaluation components of this body because they might inhibit the frank exchanges central to the peer review. Instead CSOs convey written opinions to, and have regular consultations with, the working group, and participate in the second phase of the onsite visits which assess whether countries are applying the anti-bribery structures they have put in place.[44] "Multistakeholder summitry"[45] in the guise of the Annual Forum completes the OECD's inventory of civil society conduits. So far, nine themed forums (see Table 5.1) have attracted 12,000 delegates from governments, universities, think tanks, and interest groups in more than 100 countries (see Table 5.2). Many envoys are first-rate. At the 2002 Annual Forum, for instance three Nobel Prize winners (Leo Esaki, Robert Mundell, and Burton Richter) meditated on humankind's twenty-first century fate. That said, disgraced former Enron chief Kenneth Lay is also amongst the annual forum's luminaries.

Given the foregoing, it is unsurprising that One World Trust applauded the OECD in 2006 as a "top performer"[46] among global organizations for the way it interacts with civil society. Scratch the veneer, however, and the changes are not as startling as they initially appear. The OECD's fancy for engaging Northern, conservative CSOs and those petitioning for business and commercial interests persists. Seventy-four percent of participants at the 2002 Annual Forum heralded from OECD countries.[47] If speakers at the forum are examined the prejudice is more pronounced. Nine-tenths of the presentations made to the Annual Forum are by emissaries from OECD countries

Table 5.1 Themes of OECD Annual Forums

Year	Theme
2000	Partnerships in the New Economy
2001	Sustainable Development and the New Economy
2002	Taking Care of the Fundamentals: Security, Equity, Education and Growth
2003	Grow, Develop, and Prosper
2004	Health of Nations
2005	Fuelling the Future: Security, Stability, Development
2006	Balancing Globalisation
2007	Innovation, Growth and Equity
2008	Climate Change, Growth, Stability

Table 5.2 Participants and speakers at OECD Annual Forums by country income grouping

	2000	2001	2002	2003	2004	2005	2006	2007	2008	Total	%
Participants	1,000	1,500	1,200	1,400	1,250	1,250	1,400	1,550	1,600	12,150	
Speakers:											
From OECD members	92	112	134	107	102	96	83	85	94	914	90.0
From non-OECD upper-middle-income/ high-income countries	8	5	7	3	3	4	5	4	5	44	4.3
From non-OECD lower-middle-income countries	4	4	9	1	4	7	9	4	2	44	4.3
From non-OECD low-income countries	4	6	4	1	1	5	1	1	0	23	2.3
Total	108	127	154	112	110	112	98	94	101	1,015	100

Source: Derived from OECD Forum Speakers List for the years cited. Available at www.oecd.org. Income groupings are drawn from The World Bank classification of countries by income (as at 13 June 2006).

(see Table 5.2); only 14 African speakers have brandished the microphone. Speakers from educational and charitable establishments slightly outnumber those from corporations and business lobbies (see Table 5.3). However, journalists typically emanate from the bastions of capitalism (regulars include correspondents from Bloomberg Television, the *Financial Times*, and the *Economist*) and the majority of those from academia are tinged with a neo-liberal hue. Furthermore, multinational enterprises are the principal sponsors of the Annual Forum. Five of the six backers of the 2008 Annual Forum (British Petroleum, Calyon Credit Agricole, Macquarie, Merck and Co., and Veolia) were multinational enterprises. The aberration was AARP, a U.S. NGO directed to the interests of those aged 50 and over. The Annual Forum is not a blunt exchange of views between diverse stakeholders but rather an event where acolytes of free-wheeling capitalism congregate to rehearse platitudes about the genius of free markets. One could portray the Annual Forum as a microcosm of Robert Cox's claim that there is a "nascent global historic bloc consisting of the most powerful corporate economic forces, their allies in government, and the variety of networks that evolve policy guidelines and propagate the ideology of globalization."[48]

Ougaard's panoramic review of the OECD's civil society cooperation unearths a similar story. Eight of the ten CSOs most rapt in OECD work are groups, notably environmental organizations, entreating the organization to place curbs on market arbitration of human activity

Table 5.3 Speakers at OECD Annual Forums by sector

	2000	2001	2002	2003	2004	2005	2006	2007	2008	Total	%
OECD	12	13	17	13	5	6	7	10	15	98	9.7
National and international politicians/officials	32	33	40	31	46	35	31	22	21	291	28.7
Corporations	24	26	20	18	14	19	15	19	20	175	17.2
Business lobbies	12	12	14	7	3	7	6	11	2	74	7.3
Media	3	5	10	16	16	17	14	11	10	102	10.0
Educational institutions	5	9	16	9	9	9	10	5	11	83	8.2
Social/charitable organizations	19	29	29	18	17	19	14	16	22	183	18.0
Other	1	0	8	0	0	0	0	0	0	9	0.9
Total	108	127	154	112	110	112	98	94	101	1015	100

Source: Derived from OECD Forum Speakers List for the years cited. Available at www.oecd.org.

(see Table 5.4). Nevertheless, he demonstrates that they are outgunned in numerical terms by organizations backing corporate interests, without including BIAC in the calculations.[49] The OECD is still indulging a slender stratum of CSOs that are generally sympathetic to the overall thrust of its philosophy. Therefore, it is doubtful whether OECD committees are realizing the benefits to normative governance. Likewise, it is improbable that OECD legal or palliative governance will be viewed as more legitimate as a consequence.

Of course, these shortcomings are not necessarily the fault of the OECD. Surveys show that agents hailing from the affluent North dominate supposedly global civil society and resource deficiencies thwart many but the leading, and almost by definition, conservative CSOs from maintaining widespread connections with international organizations.[50] Furthermore, the stigma from collaborating with "the capitalist club" spooks the more rebellious elements of civil society and prevents them working with the OECD. The OECD's decision to err on the side of caution when it comes to civil society may again reflect the need to walk the tightrope between appeasing criticisms of opacity and illegitimacy while avoiding the paralysis that might result from having a throng of competing viewpoints and maintaining some seclusion to ensure forthright committee discussions. In other ways, however, the OECD and its committees are culpable for the prevailing biases. They have shrewdly selected their civil society interlocutors and their points of entry. While there is a respectable sprinkling of civil society linkages

Table 5.4 Top ten civil society organizations cited in the OECD's inventory of cooperative work with civil society.

Civil society organization	Count
Business and Industry Advisory Committee	57
Trade Union Advisory Committee	55
OECD Watch	19
Consumers International	10
World Wildlife Fund	10
European Environmental Bureau	7
Transparency International	7
OXFAM	5
Greenpeace International	4
International Chamber of Commerce	4

Source: Derived from OECD, *OECD's Cooperative Work with Civil Society* C/ INF(2006)24 (Paris: OECD, 2006) in Morten Ougaard, "The OECD's Global Role," Paper presented at the workshop "Mechanisms of OECD Governance–International Incentives for National Policy Making?" University of Bremen, 21–22 September 2007.

in areas such as trade, agriculture, and the environment, the economic committees, the bellwethers of OECD policies, are almost impervious to civil society interlopers. TUAC, despite being the second most integrated CSO in the OECD's work (see Table 5.4), grumbles about the EDRC's one-eyed stance leading to recommendations lacking sufficient sensitivity to the social aspects of economic wellbeing.[51] Webb's work on the OECD's harmful tax competition initiative uncovered evidence of the Committee on Fiscal Affairs methodically consulting cabals congenial to neo-liberalism while studiously snubbing those that were not, which "from the perspective of critical groups which struggle to get any hearing at all in the OECD, this is equivalent to consulting with the fox about policies to protect the henhouse."[52] Similarly, OECD Watch

> believes that the legitimate expectations of civil society groups that participated in the 2000 revision of the Guidelines have not been met as far as the implementation procedures are concerned. OECD Watch also believes that the scope of the Guidelines is continually being eroded, seemingly at the behest of business confederations and certain governments[53] [and that there has been] a retreat in effective access for NGOs in recent years.[54]

To sum up, the OECD appears to be leaning toward complex multilateralism. How these trends evolve will depend significantly on Angel

Gurria, because the dispositions of executive-heads of international organizations are a crucial variable determining how the bodies they lead relate to civil society.[55] CSOs pushing to retrench neo-liberalism bridled at Gurria's anointment because of his track record as part of the Mexican team of NAFTA negotiators and as Mexico's finance minister where the austerity measures he introduced earned him the moniker "Señor scissor-hands."[56] Moreover, he was the only pretender for the Secretary-Generalship who refused to share his views on labor and social affairs with TUAC.[57] On the other hand, Gurria actively participates in several NGOs including the Population Council, the Center for Global Development, the World Water Council's Task Force on Financing Water for All (which he chairs), and laces his speeches with references to sharing the fruits of globalization.[58] Two years into his reign, however, and CSOs are unconvinced. OECD Watch argues that "civil society will take some persuading that under Mr Gurria's leadership the OECD really is moving beyond its traditional ethos—an exclusive club for the wealthy—and becoming 'a hub of globalization' that aims to increase well-being and prosperity for all."[59]

The OECD–G8 nexus

The accomplishments of the G8 system rest heavily on meticulous preparation and follow-up activities to maintain the momentum between their spasmodic meetings.[60] The G8 entrusts the onus to liaisons of sherpas (personal assistants to G8 leaders) and, increasingly, since the end of the Cold War, other international organizations.[61] Some insist that the G8 would operate more efficiently and effectively if it had a permanent secretariat for these purposes[62] and that complementarities in orientation and style leave the OECD ideally situated to discharge this function.[63] From the point of view of cognitive and normative governance, the G8 and the OECD are beacons of capitalism and democracy for the less enlightened world to copy and rely exclusively on the soft power of peer pressure to advance their agenda. Moreover, whereas G8 leaders and ministerial groupings assemble only periodically, the OECD is "an international economic conference in permanent session"[64] whose ongoing processes of information gathering, committee discussion, and peer review taper the fissures amongst G8 countries to a point where face-to-face negotiations between leaders or ministers can bridge them. For example, discussions in the OECD Trade Committee narrowed gaps between the then G7 countries over a recipe for commencing agricultural negotiations in the

GATT. Although talks at the OECD's 1990 MCM did not resolve the dispute, they did provide the foundation for the blueprint settled upon at the G7's Houston Summit six weeks later.[65]

As Chapter 1 documented, once they overcame their initial trepidation, G8 and OECD interactions mushroomed. Burgeoning references to, endorsements of, and requests for, work from the OECD in G8 documentation (see Table 5.5) in part reflect the expansion of the G8 system and the verbosity of the communiqués, but also indicate the extent to which the two bodies intersect across a range of policy matters. Nevertheless, split allegiances meant the OECD's dealings with the G8 system "were close but often uneasy."[66] Johnston complained that during his stint as Secretary-General the G8 sometimes neglected the OECD's proficiencies for palliative governance. He quotes the Digital Opportunity Task Force established by the Okinawa Summit of 2000 to enable developing countries to get a windfall from IT, "where the OECD was best placed to co-ordinate the follow-up; yet the responsibility was dispersed to other organizations with less expertise."[67] Furthermore, while the G8 invited leaders of commensurate international organizations (including the IEA, one of the OECD's semi-autonomous bodies) to the summit almost from the start, it took 32 years until the Heiligendamm Summit of 2007 for the OECD Secretary-General to participate in their annual jamboree.

Table 5.5 References to the OECD in G7/8 summit and ministerial communiqués.

	1st cycle (1975–81)	2nd cycle (1982–88)	3rd cycle (1989–95)	4th cycle (1996–2002)	5th cycle (2003 to date*)
Reference to OECD work or act	0	0	6	62	50
Endorsement of OECD work	7	8	16	64	24
Endorse and ask OECD to intensify efforts	0	1	6	15	17
Urge OECD to act	0	0	7	23	10
Pledge to cooperate with/in OECD	5	5	2	20	11
Total	12	14	37	184	112

Note: *July 2008
Source: Derived from G7/8 communiqués published by the University of Toronto G8 Information Centre, available online at www.g8.utoronto.ca/ (Accessed 1 August 2008).

The 2007 Heiligendamm Summit is the high watermark of G8–OECD relations. Documentation released during the summit made 36 references to the OECD's work, almost three times as many as any previous G8 heads of state meeting. The communiqué endorsed or asked the OECD to redouble its efforts with regard to intellectual property rights, counterfeiting and piracy, restrictions on foreign investment, instruments to aid failing states, and the monitoring of pledges made by the G8 to heighten Africa's capacity to trade. The G8 promised to conspire with the OECD, WHO and Global Health Workforce Alliance to refine the available data on migration of health care workers, asked the OECD to work jointly with UNCTAD and developing economies to cultivate best practices to increase foreign investment and sustainable development, and to collaborate with the ILO and the Global Compact to compose a directory of corporate responsibility. The heads of state encouraged emerging economies to become more absorbed into the OECD's networks on scientific research and technological innovation and to implement the OECD Declaration on International Investment and Multinational Enterprises. They proclaimed their willingness to promote the OECD's Risk Awareness Tool for Multinational Enterprises in Weak Governance Zones, and undertook to adhere to eminent OECD legal Acts including the OECD Principles of Corporate Governance, the anti-bribery convention, and aid-untying guidelines.

The most important announcement, however, related to the G8's informal dialogue with the governments of the Outreach-5 (O-5), Brazil, China, India, Mexico, and South Africa. Following consultations with the O-5 at Heiligendamm the G8 "decided to launch a new form of specific cooperation with major emerging economies in order to discuss substantive topics in a comprehensive follow-up process with the aim of reaching tangible results in two years" and "ask the OECD to provide a platform for such a dialogue process."[68] The dialogue concentrates on four areas:

- strategies to encourage research and safeguard innovation;
- removing barriers to cross-border investment by refining and upholding agreed codes of corporate social responsibility;
- acknowledging mutual responsibility for global development, especially in Africa, and to reinforce cooperation to attain the MDGs;
- pooling intelligence on energy efficiency and technological cooperation to reduce carbon dioxide emissions and fight climate change.[69]

In July 2007, the OECD Council sanctioned the Heiligendamm Dialogue Process Support Unit. Stationed within the office of the Secretary-General, the unit is led by Ulrich Benterbusch, Germany's onetime sous-Sherpa to the G8, and is staffed by four policy analysts, each attached to a working group dealing with an aspect of the dialogue. Drawing upon the expertise of the OECD directorates, the unit's duty is to prepare working group meetings.

The Heiligendamm Summit and the dialogue with which it is synonymous depart from previous demands made of the OECD by the G8 because of the assortment of topics that are simultaneously involved and the resources being thrown at the process. It is therefore worth surmising what impact the Heiligendamm Process might have on the OECD–G8 nexus. A positive perspective pictures the Heiligendamm Process as another opportunity for dialogue to socialize key non-member economies with the norms and values associated with the G8–OECD world. Mutual distrust and misunderstanding are formidable hurdles to cooperation between the established and emerging powers, and "it is hoped that the informal atmosphere of Heiligendamm Dialogue Process working groups, through exchanges rather than negotiations, will facilitate rapprochement."[70] Such quiet diplomacy is the thing for which the OECD is renowned. If by its maneuvering of the Heiligendamm Process the OECD helps to instill the O-5 with the democratic and capitalist values they sometimes lack, these countries will become fit for membership of the G8–OECD society. From this upbeat angle, the Heiligendamm Process will reinforce the enhanced engagement program, accelerating the accessions of systemically important economies. Moreover, as the handmaiden of the transition of the Western-dominated international institutions of the twentieth century to those representing the balance of power in the twenty-first century, the OECD's star would be in the ascendant. The Heiligendamm Process might therefore be another steppingstone to solemnizing the G8–OECD relationship and presenting the OECD with a sheltered niche in global governance.

The hitch with this cheerful depiction is that a wondrous outcome from the Heiligendamm Process is far from assured. The anodyne interim report on the Heiligendamm Process presented at the 2008 G8 Hokkaido Summit suggests the working groups are yet to achieve anything of substance.[71] Speaking after Hokkaido, one Japanese diplomat confided that the G8-O-5's shared grasp of Heiligendamm topics may even be deteriorating, insinuating that their conflicts over climate change and the environment "may soon resemble management and labor stand-offs at their worst."[72] This is a function of a second dilemma, namely that rather than being a dialogue where G8 and O-5 countries learn from each other as they would in other OECD contexts, outpourings from leading OECD members have led the Heiligendamm Process to be construed as a conduit for indoctrinating the O-5. The German ambassador to the OECD asserted that the Heiligendamm Process

> must drive home the message that market-oriented rules, together with a social concept of globalization and a sustainable approach to resource management, are preconditions for global development and prosperity. It is in this context that we wish to come to an understanding with our partners on the core challenges facing the global economy.[73]

In other words, the Heiligendamm Process allows ideas to flow from the G8 to the O-5 but offers negligible opportunities for them to flow in reverse. Disaffection with the Heiligendamm Process could spill over into and damage the OECD's enhanced engagement program in which four of the O-5 participate. The incongruities of the O-5 and enhanced engagement program are potential source of friction. Mexico is the only member of the O-5 that belongs to the OECD, while Indonesia participates in the enhanced engagement program but lies outside the O-5. Lastly, as a socializing tool, the Heiligendamm Process founders on the same faults as the enhanced engagement program. Specifically, O-5 countries display only halfhearted enthusiasm for entering clubs purporting to represent the world's advanced societies, therefore dangling the carrot of G8 or OECD membership in front of them is unlikely to wring radical changes from their behavior and outlook. This is especially the case given the abbreviated nature of the Heiligendamm Process, which is timetabled to finish by the 2009 G8 summit.

Away from the inadequacies of the Heiligendamm Process, opposition to the idea in both forums makes the OECD's emergence as a permanent G8 secretariat implausible at present. Part of the rationale for founding the G8 system was to emancipate political leaders from the constraints imposed by the bureaucratization of international politics. Consequently, the G8 leaders have consistently repudiated plans to lumber the system with a permanent secretariat.[74] Contemporaneously, senior officials in the OECD quake over the effects that becoming a permanent G8 secretariat would have on the organization's operational independence. Privately, a number of smaller OECD members echo this unease and recoil at the G8's "almost hierarchical relationship"[75] with the OECD which means the interests of G8 countries already control the organization's agenda to an unacceptable degree. Discrepancies in G8 and OECD membership also pose difficulties. Could and would non-OECD members of the G8 draw upon the secretariat? Finally, as the OECD scrabbles to subdue indictments about its illegitimacy, members and staffers have reservations about becoming exaggeratedly entangled with a G8 that is seen at best as an irreverent "global hot tub party"[76] or "ritualized photo opportunity"[77] and at worst a malign epicenter of global governance peddling policies that provide for the opulence and stability of its members and close allies while condemning the bulk of humanity to impoverishment, instability, and insecurity.[78]

Conclusion

This chapter began by asserting that reform was essential to "securing the future"[79] of the OECD. Under Donald Johnston, and latterly Angel Gurria, OECD reform is in full swing. Five accession processes are underway, the enhanced engagement process is cajoling cooperation between the OECD and the emergent powers of the global South, civil society entanglements are healthier than ever, and the organization is increasingly the institution of choice for a whole range of the G8 system's follow-up activities. Nevertheless, this is not enough to appease those who chide the OECD's irrelevance or illegitimacy. They point to the continued absence of several systemically important economies, the dominance of conservative civil society groups, and, although their relations are at a high water*mark*, lurking distrust between the G8 and the wider OECD community means it is too early to talk of a water*shed* in OECD–G8 relations.

The indications are that the OECD is set to address this by a process of forceful enlargement, further outreach to non-members and civil society, and, if Gurria gets his way, hopping into the G8's marsupial pouch. Whatever happens, the OECD must manage three contradictions inherent in the reform strategy if it is not to become self-defeating. First, the OECD must balance a desire for inclusivity with the pitfall of inflexibility. As James Salzman, a former OECD employee, comments with regard to civil society, the OECD is diffident on this issue, "the result is an organization whose administrative safeguards are in flux—struggling over how much and what types of engagement with non-state actors are necessary without undermining the organization's basic mission."[80] The OECD needs to welcome new participants (be they states or CSOs) while ensuring they do not choke the agenda or devastate the organization's much admired working methods. Second, there is likemindedness versus legitimacy. Winning legitimacy by accepting the Big Six or allowing carte blanche access to CSOs is futile if it prevents the achievement of a workable consensus. Finally, particularly with the G8 in mind, there is certainty versus constraint. Hitching the OECD to the G8 steed would give the organization a protected place in the anatomy of global governance, but at the cost of constraining the organization's autonomy.

6 The future of the OECD

When in 1948 U.S. Congressional representatives insisted upon a permanent organization to underpin George Marshall's eponymous plan, nobody foresaw that these arrangements would endure for over 60 years, outliving (and eventually enveloping) some of their communist foes to become a cornerstone of the liberal democratic order. If the confinement of the OEEC and OECD were products of specific historical junctures, their survival is no accident. Under the umbrella of U.S. hegemony, leading states sought to build a new liberal democratic order.

This order aimed to reap the benefits of market exchange while maintaining the autonomy states needed to deliver domestic welfare policies and protect their citizens from the worst excesses of free market capitalism. In the febrile postwar atmosphere, parenting a liberal democratic order was not a straightforward undertaking. One of the keys to its success was institutions like the IMF, GATT, OEEC, and OECD where states agreed on rules, norms and principles to guide, within certain limits, the liberalization of their economies. As responsible parents, states did not desert their offspring but sought through these international organizations to screen it from infection and disease (such as trade protectionism and restrictions on the circulation of capital), tame its teenage tantrums (the oil crises and stagflation), and imbue it with suitable values for adulthood (democracy, capitalism, and the rule of law). Pundits of a "hyperglobalist" disposition extend this analogy, claiming that with the reintegration of national economies and the ascendancy of neo-liberalism the international order has flown the nest and pays little heed to the rules laid down by the states or international organizations that conceived it.[1] Most commentators deride this view however, and think that states, individually or collectively, are vital players with the power, returning to the definition of global governance offered in the introductory chapter, to "manage our collective affairs."[2]

This final chapter conjectures about the OECD's future role in the management of humankind's collective affairs. While pessimistic portraits of a senescent OECD drifting into quiet obscurity are plausible, on balance this author is inclined toward a more sanguine scenario where an evolving OECD continues to play a significant, if spectral, role in twenty-first century global governance. The OECD's imperfections notwithstanding, there are six grounds for optimism.

First, just as the interdependence propagated by the OEEC justified its transfiguration into the OECD to tend it, so the globalization propagated by the OECD justifies its existence. If the OECD did not exist, states would create something akin to it. In a globalizing world, the levels of interconnectedness between developed states, and increasingly between them and their developing counterparts, means states need more than ever a venue where they can informally evolve agreed norms and rules or agree to take coordinated action to underpin the management of our collective affairs. The queue of countries waiting to join the organization and the fact that there are no absconders reflects this. Nowhere are the realities of interdependence and the futilities of trying to pursue an independent approach better symbolized than in the communities of influence centered on the OECD committee system. It is difficult to think of any significant policy arena *without* an international dimension. Even topics like health and education, traditionally construed as exclusively domestic concerns have, with the rise of medical tourism, the migration of health workers, and student mobility, acquired an cross-border dimension. Furthermore, the development at the OECD of ways to compare the health and education standards cross-nationally exposes weaknesses in domestic policies.

Naturally, there are other venues where states can and do pursue the management of collective affairs. The nebulous nature of the OECD's remit means its roles are prone to appropriation by one of the veritable galaxy of mechanisms populating contemporary global governance. This can occur because of the debilities as well as the strengths of other bodies. The IMF, a "bystander during the credit crunch,"[3] is culling staff and hawking its gold reserves, leading one commentator to adduce "its future role may be more as an expert economic adviser"[4] putting it in direct competition with the OECD. Moreover, because the OECD bestrides subjects beholden to many different government agencies the organization lacks clear ownership in national capitals.[5] Rather than sweating over this, the OECD makes a virtue of it. The fact that it is not in hock to single government departments, especially central banks and finance ministries, confers the pliability needed to meet the caprices of its patrons. The OECD is also adept at carving out niches and spying linkages between seemingly disparate topics. The OECD is an international organization of "firsts": the first to institute a comprehensive system of peer review, the first to apply a legal instrument to capital movements,[6] the first to have a dedicated environment directorate, and the first to examine a series of specific issues in a systematic fashion. This "chameleon-like"[7] quality helps to explain the OECD's longevity and, in a world of increasing complexity, is the second cause for optimism about the organization's prospects.

Third, as the previous paragraph intimates, other international organizations are no more surefooted than the OECD. The Bretton Woods institutions and the G8 are as susceptible as the OECD to indictments of cronyism, illegitimacy, and ineffectiveness.[8] The threats to the OECD from entities such as the G20 finance ministers and central bank governors are overstated. Countermanding the G20's geographical appeal as home to most of the world's leading powers, is that functionally the G20 is a one-trick pony concerned exclusively with promoting global financial stability. Nothing stops the G20's remit expanding, equivalent G20 get-togethers surfacing to peruse other policy issues, or a prospective "L20" for the leaders of these 20 countries emerging. Anne-Marie Slaughter thinks the G20 "could be a global think tank, a caucus in many existing institutions, a catalyst for networked global governance operating through national government officials."[9] The question is whether it could do this without the logistical support and institutional memory of a large and expensive secretariat. Besides balking at the cost of a secretariat the G20, reminiscent of the G8 genus, will contest the bureaucratization of their meetings. That the OECD typically complements rather than competes with other international bodies is a fourth reason for optimism.[10] The OECD positions itself upstream and downstream of these institutions, resolving gridlocks prior to their meetings and taking work forward in their aftermath. A boisterous and assertive G20 plus other additions to the "gaggle of G's" afford another outlet for the OECD's palliative governance, especially if the submersion of the systemically significant G20 economies in OECD work continues through the enlargement and outreach strategy.

Fifth, the OECD's techniques and temperament will give it certain comparative advantages over a longer time horizon. Predictions that soft law and soft power will be the "means to success in world politics"[11] lead some commentators to envisage the OECD as the archetype for future international organizations.[12] Various international organizations, including those such as the IMF and EU that have material sanctions at their disposal, mimic the OECD's peer review and surveillance processes and rely on moral suasion to shape their members' behavior. This is not to say "hard power" mechanisms are moribund but to recognize that states are concerned to maintain their reputation amongst their peers by ensuring their actions are consistent with norms generated by the community to which they belong. The uproar in countries performing poorly in the PISA survey and the hostile responses by those labeled by the OECD as a "harmful" tax havens are merely two examples of the importance of the normative dimensions of OECD governance. The OECD method also involves national officials to a degree unmatched by other international organizations. The OECD's transgovernmental spirit may beguile those that condemn international organizations as undemocratic and unaccountable. Rather than being the products of a faceless secretariat, officials from national governments develop and implement OECD recommendations on the authority of their political overlords. In turn, citizens can hold politicians accountable through the democratic processes prevailing in OECD countries. Next, the OECD is one of the few genuinely multidisciplinary international organizations, enabling it to comprehend conventionally compartmentalized policy domains. As the organization's 2008 *Annual Report* remarks, "the OECD's strength lies in its ability to help governments solve complex problems by addressing the multiplicity of dimensions that characterize today's global challenges."[13]

Sixth, apart from some stoutly refuted allegations about nepotism and a lack of transparency in some senior appointments and the spiraling costs of the refurbishment of the OECD's headquarters,[14] Angel Gurria is proving an astute and energetic Secretary-General. Taking the reform baton from Donald Johnston, Gurria's OECD has launched accession negotiations with five prospective members and deepened engagement with non-members and civil society. Additionally, he has shaken up the committee system and secured several important responsibilities for the OECD, including acting as the platform for the Heiligendamm Process, a handshake between the dominant countries of the twentieth century and those perched to dominate the twenty-first. This augurs well for the remaining challenges Gurria and his contemporaries must face down if this rosy future scenario is to happen. The hardest challenge, doubtless, is hooking up with the O-5 countries without incinerating the OECD's ability to deliver its core mission of promoting policies to achieve the highest levels of sustainable economic growth. If the OECD's hierarchy can do so, the heyday of this enigmatic organization may yet be to come.

Notes

Foreword

1 Francis Fukuyama, *The End of History and the Last Man* (London: Penguin, 1992).
2 See Bernard M. Hoekman and Petros C. Mavroidis, *The World Trade Organization: Law, Economics, and Politics* (London: Routledge, 2007); also Rorden Wilkinson, *The WTO: Crisis and the Governance of Global Trade* (London: Routledge, 2006).
3 Michael Schechter, *United Nations Global Conferences* (London: Routledge, 2005).
4 See, for example, Andrew Baker, David Hudson, and Richard Woodward, *Governing Financial Globalization: International Political Economy and Multi-level Governance* (London: Routledge, 2005); Simon Lee and Richard Woodward, "Implementing the Third Way: The Delivery of Public Services under the Blair Government," in *Public Money and Management* 22, no. 4 (October–December 2002): 49–56; and Richard Woodward, "Global Monitor: The Organisation for Economic Cooperation and Development," in *New Political Economy* 9, no. 1 (March 2004): 113–27.

Introduction

1 OECD, *Annual Report 2005* (Paris: OECD, 2005), 7.
2 See Richard Woodward, "Governance and the Organisation for Economic Cooperation and Development," in *Global Governance and Japan: The Institutional Architecture*, ed. Glenn D. Hook and Hugo Dobson (London: Routledge, 2007), 59–75.
3 Robert G. Gilpin, *The Challenge of Global Capitalism: The World Economy in the 21st Century* (Princeton, N.J.: Princeton University Press, 2000), 184; Miriam Camps, *"First World" Relationships: The Role of the OECD* (Paris: The Atlantic Institute for International Affairs, 1975), 10.
4 OECD, *Annual Report 2005*, 6.
5 World Bank, *World Development Report 2007: Development and the Next Generation* (Washington, D.C.: World Bank, 2006), 287.
6 UNDP, *Human Development Report 2007/2008: Fighting Climate Change: Human Solidarity in a Divided World* (New York: UNDP, 2007), 230–32.
7 See Richard Woodward, "The Organisation for Economic Cooperation and Development," *New Political Economy* 9, no. 1 (March 2004): 114.

8 OECD, "Convention on the Organisation for Economic Cooperation and Development," available at www.oecd.org/document/7/0,2340,en_2649_201 185_1915847_1_1_1_1,00.html (Accessed 31 August 2008).

9 James Salzman, "Labor Rights, Globalization and Institutions: The Role and Influence of the Organization for Economic Cooperation and Development," *Michigan Journal of International Law* 21, no. 4 (Summer 2000): 777.

10 The Commission on Global Governance, *Our Global Neighbourhood: The Report of the Commission on Global Governance* (Oxford: Oxford University Press, 1995), 2.

11 Margaret P. Karns and Karen A. Mingst, *International Organizations: The Politics and Processes of Global Governance* (Boulder, Colo.: Lynne Rienner, 2004).

12 Nicholas Bayne, *Hanging in There: The G7 and G8 Summit in Maturity and Renewal* (Aldershot: Ashgate, 2000), 48.

13 Nicholas Bayne, "Making Sense of Western Economic Policies: The Role of the OECD," *World Today* 43, no. 2 (February 1987): 27.

14 Camps, *"First World" Relationships*, 10.

15 Martin Marcussen, "OECD Governance through Soft Law," in *Soft Law in Governance and Regulation: An Interdisciplinary Analysis*, ed. Ulrika Morth (Cheltenham: Edward Elgar, 2004); Per-Olof Busch, "The OECD Environment Directorate: The Art of Persuasion and its Limitations," *GlobGov Global Governance Working Paper no. 20—October 2006*; Salzman, "Labor Rights, Globalization and Institutions: The Role and Influence of the Organization for Economic Cooperation and Development," 769–848.

16 See for example OECD, *A Strategy for Enlargement and Outreach: Report by the Chair of the Heads of Delegation Working Group on the Enlargement Strategy and Outreach, Ambassador Seiichiro Noburu* (OECD: Paris, 2004), 16.

17 Tony Porter and Michael Webb, "The Role of the OECD in the Orchestration of Global Knowledge Networks," paper presented to the 45th Annual Convention of the International Studies Association, Montreal, Canada, 17–20 March 2004, 3.

18 Richard N. Cooper, "International Cooperation in Public Health as a Prologue to Macroeconomic Cooperation," *Brookings Discussion Papers in International Economics*, no. 44 (1986).

19 Marcussen, "OECD Governance through Soft Law," 106.

20 Salzman, "Labor Rights, Globalization and Institutions: The Role and Influence of the Organization for Economic Cooperation and Development," 832.

21 Scott Sullivan, *From War to Wealth: Fifty Years of Innovation* (Paris: OECD, 1997), 6.

22 Morten Ougaard, *Political Globalization: State, Power and Social Forces* (Basingstoke: Palgrave, 2004), 86.

23 Robert Wolfe, "The Organization for Economic Cooperation and Development," in *Routledge Encyclopedia of International Political Economy*, ed. R. J. Barry Jones (London: Routledge, 2001), 1180.

24 Marcussen, "OECD Governance through Soft Law," 106.

25 James Rosenau, "Strong Demand, Huge Supply: Governance in an Emerging Epoch," in *Multi-level Governance*, ed. Ian Bache and Matthew Flinders (Oxford: Oxford University Press, 2004), 31–49.

1 Origin and evolution

1 OECD, "Chair's summary of the OECD Council at Ministerial Level, Paris, 23–24 May 2006—Delivering Prosperity," available at www.oecd.org/document/43/0,3343,en_21571361_36330557_36781483_1_1_1_1,00.html (Accessed 3 July 2007).

2 Robert Wolfe, "From Reconstructing Europe to Constructing Globalization: the OECD in Historical Perspective," in *The OECD and Transnational Governance*, ed. Rianne Mahon and Stephen McBride (Vancouver, Canada: UBC Press, 2008), 28.

3 George H. W. Bush, "Address before a Joint Session of the Congress on the Persian Gulf Crisis and the Federal Budget Deficit," available at http://bushlibrary.tamu.edu/research/public_papers.php?id = 2217&year = 1990& month = 9 (Accessed 20 November 2008).

4 "Mr X" [George F. Kennan] "The Sources of Soviet Conduct," *Foreign Affairs* 25, no. 4 (July 1947): 575.

5 Anonymous, "Documents on War and Transitional Organizations: Convention for European Economic Cooperation, Signed at Paris, April 16, 1948," in *International Organization* 2, no. 2 (June 1948): 420–26.

6 On the origins of the OEEC see Lincoln Gordon, "The Organization for European Economic Cooperation," *International Organization* 10, no. 1 (February 1956): 1–4; Alan S. Milward, *The Reconstruction of Western Europe, 1945–51* (London: Methuen, 1984).

7 Milward, *The Reconstruction of Western Europe 1945–51*, 168–211.

8 Our Paris Correspondent, "OEEC's Tenth Birthday," *Economist* 187, no. 5982 (19–25 January 1958): 218.

9 See William Diebold, *Trade and Payments in Western Europe: A Study in Economic Cooperation 1947–51* (New York: Harper & Brothers, 1952).

10 OEEC, *Twelfth Annual Economic Review* (Paris: OEEC, 1961), 185.

11 OECD Observer, "Twenty Nations Exchange Their Policy Ideas for Mutual Economic Benefit," *OECD Observer* no. 3 (March 1963): 4.

12 Michael Palmer and John Lambert et al., eds, *European Unity: A Survey of the European Institutions* (London: George Allen & Unwin, 1968), 109.

13 Thomas C. Schelling, "American Foreign Assistance," *World Politics* 7, no. 4 (July 1955): 619.

14 OEEC, *A Decade of Co-operation: Achievements and Perspectives: 9th report of the O.E.E.C.* (Paris: OEEC, 1958), 111–26.

15 Henry G. Aubrey, *Atlantic Economic Cooperation: The Case of the OECD* (New York: Frederick A. Praeger, 1967), 10, 13; Miriam Camps, *"First World" Relationships: The Role of The OECD* (Paris: The Atlantic Institute for International Affairs, 1975), 11.

16 See Emile Benoit, *Europe at Sixes and Sevens: The Common Market, the Free Trade Association and the United States* (New York: Columbia University Press, 1961).

17 See Theodore H. Cohn, *Governing Global Trade: International Institutions in Conflict and Convergence* (Aldershot: Ashgate, 2002), 40–41; Michael Palmer and John Lambert et al., eds, *European Unity: A Survey of the European Institutions*, 109–10.

18 Robert Putnam and Nicholas Bayne, *Hanging Together: Cooperation and Conflict in the Seven-Power Summits (2nd edition)* (London: Sage, 1987), 25.

19 Thorkil Kristensen, "Five Years of O.E.C.D.," in *European Yearbook Volume XIII*, ed. The Council of Europe (The Hague, The Netherlands: Martinus Nijhoff, 1967), 105 (emphasis in original).

20 Martin Marcussen, "The OECD in Search of a Role: Playing the Idea Game," Paper presented at the European Consortium for Political Research, Grenoble, 6–11 April 2001, 1.

21 Robert W. Russell, "Transgovernmental Interaction in the International Monetary System, 1960–72," *International Organization* 27, no. 4 (Autumn 1973): 439; Stanley Fischer, "International Macroeconomic Policy Coordination," in *International Economic Cooperation*, ed. Martin Feldstein (Chicago, Ill.: University of Chicago Press, 1988), 27.

22 Russell, "Transgovernmental Interaction in the International Monetary System, 1960–72," 456.

23 John S. Odell, *U.S. International Monetary Policy: Markets, Power and Ideas as Sources of Change* (Princeton, N.J.: Princeton University Press, 1982), 349–50; Russell, "Transgovernmental Interaction in the International Monetary System, 1960–72," 456–59.

24 Cohn, *Governing Global Trade: International Institutions in Conflict and Convergence*, 43.

25 Aubrey, *Atlantic Economic Cooperation: The Case of the OECD*, 90.

26 John W. Evans, *The Kennedy Round in American Trade Policy: The Twilight of the GATT?* (Cambridge, Mass.: Harvard University Press, 1971), 248.

27 OECD, *Annual Report 2006* (Paris: OECD, 2006), 111.

28 Goran Ohlin, "The Organization for Economic Cooperation and Development," *International Organization* 22, no. 1 (Winter 1968): 239; OECD Observer, "International Technical Cooperation: Evaluation and Perspectives," *OECD Observer* no. 29 (August 1967): 4.

29 OECD Observer, "The High-Level Meeting of the OECD Development Assistance Committee," *OECD Observer* no. 18 (October 1965): 3.

30 Thorkil Kristensen, "OECD in the Years to Come," *OECD Observer* no. 24 (October 1966): 6; Ohlin, "The Organization for Economic Cooperation and Development," 236.

31 Emile van Lennep, "The Interdependence of Nations and the Peace of Canada," Address to the Joint Meeting of The Canadian Club of Toronto and The Empire Club of Canada, 22 October 1973.

32 Sullivan, *From War to Wealth: Fifty Years of Innovation* (Paris: OECD, 1997), 39.

33 See Richard Scott, *The History of the International Energy Agency: The First 20 Years—Volume One: Origins and Structure* (Paris: OECD/IEA, 1994).

34 Robert O. Keohane, *After Hegemony: Cooperation and Discord in the World Political Economy* (Princeton, N.J.: Princeton University Press, 1984), 224–31.

35 Richard Scott, *The History of the International Energy Agency: The First 20 Years—Volume Two: Major Policies and Actions* (Paris: OECD/IEA, 1994), 133–47; Richard Scott, *The History of the International Energy Agency: The First 30 Years—Volume Four: Supplement to Volumes I, II, and III* (Paris: OECD/IEA, 2004), 187–92; OECD, *Annual Report 2006*, 92.

36 Richard Scott, *The History of the International Energy Agency: The First 30 Years—Volume Four*, 195–245.

37 Robert Wolfe, *The Making of the Peace, 1993: The OECD in Canadian Economic Diplomacy* (Kingston, Canada: Queen's University, 1993), 43.

38 William J. Drake and Kalypso Nicolaidis, "Ideas, Interests and Institutionalization: 'Trade in Services' and the Uruguay Round," *International Organization* 46, no. 1 (Winter 1992): 41–53.
39 Ronald K. Shelp, "Trade in Services," *Foreign Policy* no. 65 (Winter 1986): 64.
40 Shelp, "Trade in Services," 72.
41 Cohn, *Governing Global Trade: International Institutions in Conflict and Convergence*, 147–53, 182–84.
42 Martin Marcussen, "The OECD in Search of a Role: Playing the Idea Game," 5–8.
43 Sullivan, *From War to Wealth*, 41.
44 Michael Webb, *The Political Economy of Policy Coordination: International Adjustment Since 1945* (Ithaca, N.Y.: Cornell University Press, 1995), 127–28, 131–33; Robert Putnam and Nicholas Bayne, *Hanging Together: Cooperation and Conflict in the Seven-Power Summits (2nd edition)*, 161.
45 See Wolfe, *The Making of the Peace, 1993*, 5, 103.
46 Camps, *"First World" Relationships: The Role of the OECD*, 29.
47 Louis W. Pauly, "The Political Foundations of Multilateral Economic Surveillance," *International Journal* 47, no. 2 (Spring 1992): 293–327.
48 Nicholas Bayne, *Hanging In There: The G7 and G8 Summit in Maturity and Renewal* (Aldershot: Ashgate, 2000), 53.
49 Yoichi Funabashi, *Managing the Dollar: From the Plaza to the Louvre* (Washington, D.C.: Institute for International Economics, 1988); Paul Krugman, *Has the Adjustment Process Worked?* (Washington, D.C.: Institute for International Economics, 1991).
50 Aubrey, *Atlantic Economic Cooperation: The Case of the OECD*, 21.
51 Alan Friedman, "OECD: an 'Unhappy' Group?" *International Herald Tribune*, 16 March 1994, available at www.iht.com/articles/1994/03/16/oecd_1.php (Accessed 20 June 2007).
52 Jean-Claude Paye, "OECD: Analyst and Catalyst," *OECD Observer* no. 44 (January 1987): 4–7.
53 Putnam and Bayne, *Hanging Together: Cooperation and Conflict in the Seven-Power Summits (2nd edition)*, 275.
54 Robert Wolfe, "From Reconstructing Europe to Constructing Globalization: The OECD in Historical Perspective," 36.
55 Bayne, *Hanging In There: The G7 and G8 Summit in Maturity and Renewal*, 55; Putnam and Bayne, *Hanging Together: Cooperation and Conflict in the Seven-Power Summits (2nd edition)*, 162.
56 Stephen Gill, "Theorizing the Interregnum: The Double Movement and Global Politics in the 1990s," in *International Political Economy: Understanding Global Disorder*, ed. Bjorn Hettne (London: Zed Books, 1995), 65–99. Morten Ougaard, *Political Globalization: State, Power and Social Forces* (Basingstoke: Palgrave, 2004), 78–80.
57 Seiichiro Noboru, Japanese ambassador to the OECD, quoted in Paul Betts, "Navigating the OECD 'supertanker'," *Financial Times*, 3 March 2003, 13.
58 Alan Friedman, "OECD: an 'Unhappy' Group?," *International Herald Tribune*, 16 March 1994.
59 Alan Friedman, "U.S. Gives Up on Forcing Out OECD Chief," *International Herald Tribune*, 26 November 1994, available at www.iht.com/articles/1994/11/26/oecd_0.php (Accessed 27 June 2008).

60 OECD, "Meeting of the Council at Ministerial Level Paris, 21–22 May 1996," available at www.g7.utoronto.ca/oecd/oecd96.htm (Accessed 27 June 2007).

61 Donald Johnston, "Statistics, knowledge and progress," *OECD Observer* no. 246–47 (December 2004–January 2005) available at www.oecdobserver. org/news/fullstory.php/aid/1514/Statistics,_knowledge_and_progress.html (Accessed 3 July 2007).

62 See OECD, *The OECD—Challenges and Strategic Objectives: 1997. Note by the Secretary General C(97)180* (Paris: OECD, 1997); OECD, *The OECD— Challenges and Strategic Objectives C(2001)240* (Paris: OECD, 2001).

63 OECD, *Council at Ministerial Level, 29–30 April 2003: Reform and Modernisation of the OECD C/MIN(2003)6* (Paris: OECD, 2003), 7.

64 OECD, *Getting to Grips with Globalisation: The OECD in a Changing World* (Paris: OECD, 2004), 27.

65 OECD, *Council at Ministerial Level, 29–30 April 2003: Reform and Modernisation of the OECD*, 4.

66 OECD, "CCNM Home: Global Forums," available at www.oecd.org/page s/0,3417,en_36335986_36339065_1_1_1_1_1,00.html (Accessed 6 July 2007).

67 OECD, *OECD Global Relations and the Role of the CCNM*, available at www.oecd.org/dataoecd/52/38/36701828.pdf (Accessed 6 July 2007); OECD, "Online Guide to Intergovernmental Activity," available at http:// webnet3.oecd.org/OECDgroups/ (Accessed 6 July 2007).

68 James Salzman, "Decentralized Administrative Law in the Organization for Economic Cooperation and Development," *Law and Contemporary Problems* 68, no. 3–4 (Summer–Autumn 2005): 200–3.

69 David Henderson, *The MAI Affair: A Story and Its Lessons* (London: Royal Institute for International Affairs, 1993), 22–34.

70 Richard Woodward, "The Organisation for Economic Cooperation and Development," *New Political Economy* 9, no. 1 (March 2004): 120.

71 Stephen J. Kobrin, "The MAI and the Clash of Globalizations," *Foreign Policy* no. 112 (Fall 1998): 97.

72 Alan Rugman, "The Political Economy of the Multilateral Agreement on Investment," available at www.g7.utoronto.ca/annual/rugman1998/index. html (Accessed 1 July 2007).

73 OECD, "OECD Forum 2000—Partnerships in the New Economy," available at www.oecd.org/document/52/0,3343,en_21571361_37578380_33614580_1_1_ 1_1,00.html (Accessed 1 July 2007).

74 Monica Blagescu and Robert Lloyd, *2006 Global Accountability Report: Holding Power to Account* (London: One World Trust, 2006), 43.

75 Richard Woodward, "Towards Complex Multilateralism? Civil Society and the OECD," in *The OECD and Transnational Governance*, ed. Rianne Mahon and Stephen McBride (Vancouver: UBC Press, 2008), 91.

76 OECD, *A Strategy for Enlargement and Outreach: Report of the Chair of the Heads of Delegation Working Group on the Enlargement Strategy and Outreach, Ambassador Seiichiro Noburu* (Paris: OECD, 2004), 16.

77 Robert Wolfe, "From Reconstructing Europe to Constructing Globalization: The OECD in Historical Perspective," 39.

78 See Michael C. Webb, "Defining the Boundaries of Legitimate State Practice: Norms, Transnational Actors and the OECD's Project on Harmful Tax Competition," *Review of International Political Economy* 11, no. 4 (October 2004): 787–827; Richard Woodward, "Offshore Strategies in

Global Political Economy: Small Islands and the Case of the EU and OECD Harmful Tax Competition Initiatives," *Cambridge Review of International Affairs* 19, no. 4 (December 2006): 688–90, 692–93.

79 Stephen McBride and Russell A. Williams, "Globalization, the Restructuring of Labour Markets and Policy Convergence: The OECD 'Jobs Strategy'," *Global Social Policy* 1, no. 3 (December 2001): 281–309.

80 For detailed biographies of the candidates see OECD, "Selection of a New Secretary-General of the OECD," available at www.oecd.org/document/17/0,3343,en_2649_201185_35062801_1_1_1_1,00.html (Accessed 23 November 2008).

81 John Authers, "Key Technocrat from Mexico Will Bring Flair to OECD Helm," *Financial Times*, 28 November 2005, 10.

82 OECD, "OECD Council Resolution on Enlargement and Enhanced Engagement," available at www.oecd.org/document/7/0,3343,en_2649_2011 85_38604487_1_1_1_1,00.html (Accessed 1 July 2007).

83 James Kanter, "Mexican Plans to Raise OECD's Low Profile," *International Herald Tribune*, 30 November 2005. Available at www.iht.com/article s/2005/11/30/business/oecd.php (Accessed 31 August 2008).

2 Organization and functioning

1 OECD, *Resolution of the Council on a New Governance Structure for the Organisation C(2006)78/FINAL* (Paris: OECD, 2006).

2 OECD, "Convention on the Organisation for Economic Cooperation and Development," available at www.oecd.org/document/7/0,2340,en_2649_201 185_1915847_1_1_1_1,00.html (Accessed 31 August 2008); OECD, *Rules of Procedure of the Organisation* (Paris: OECD, 1992). These rules are currently undergoing revision to reflect alterations to the OECD's governance structure. Upon completion, they will be available from the Legal Affairs section of the OECD website.

3 OECD, "European Community," available at www.oecd.org/about/0,3347, en_33873108_33873325_1_1_1_1_1,00.html (Accessed 3 March 2008).

4 OECD, *Supplementary Protocol No. 1 to the Convention on the OECD* (Paris: OECD, 1960), 1.

5 Robert Wolfe, *The Making of the Peace, 1993: The OECD in Canadian Economic Diplomacy* (Kingston, Canada: Queen's University, 1993), 28–29.

6 OECD, *Resolution of the Council on a New Governance Structure for the Organisation*, 6–10.

7 OECD, *OECD: History, Aims, Structure* (Paris: OECD, 1971), 35.

8 E-mail correspondence with the OECD (5 March 2008).

9 David Henderson, "The Role of the OECD in Liberalising International Trade and Capital Flows," *The World Economy* 19, no. 5 (September 1996): 14 (my emphasis).

10 OECD, "On-Line Guide to OECD Intergovernmental Activity," available at http://www2.oecd.org/oecdgroups/ (Accessed 1 July 2008).

11 OECD, *Annual Report 2008* (Paris: OECD, 2008), 100.

12 OECD, "OECD Committee Information Service OLISnet Background Briefing Presentation," available at www.oecd.org/dataoecd/9/6/35895935.pdf (Accessed 2 July 2008).

13 See OECD, *Resolution of the Council Concerning the Participation of Non-Members in the Work of Subsidiary Bodies of the Organisation C(2004)132/ FINAL* (Paris: OECD, 2004).

14 OECD, "On-Line Guide to OECD Intergovernmental Activity."

15 TUAC, "Trade Union Advisory Committee to the OECD," available at www.tuac.org/en/public/index.phtml (Accessed 27 March 2008).

16 BIAC, "About BIAC," available at www.biac.org/aboutus.htm (Accessed 27 March 2008).

17 TUAC, "About TUAC," available at www.tuac.org/en/public/tuac/index.phtml (Accessed 27 March 2008); BIAC, "About BIAC."

18 For an inventory of OECD surveillance practices see Fabrizio Pagani, *Peer Review: A Tool for Cooperation and Change. An Analysis of an OECD Working Method* (Paris: OECD, 2002), 15–21.

19 OECD, *Policy Brief: Peer Review: a Tool for Co-operation and Change*, available at www.oecd.org/dataoecd/9/41/37922614.pdf (Accessed 3 July 2008), 3–5.

20 Pagani, *Peer Review*, 10–11.

3 A framework for understanding

1 Morten Ougaard, *Political Globalization: State, Power and Social Forces* (Basingstoke: Palgrave, 2004), 82.

2 Martin Marcussen, "OECD Governance through Soft Law," in *Soft Law in Governance and Regulation: an Interdisciplinary Analysis*, ed. Ulrika Morth (Cheltenham: Edward Elgar, 2004), 120–23.

3 OECD, *A Strategy for Enlargement and Outreach: Report by the Chair of the Heads of Delegation Working Group on the Enlargement Strategy and Outreach, Ambassador Seiichiro Noboru* (Paris: OECD, 2004), 7.

4 See for example Thorkil Kristensen, "OECD in the Years to Come," *OECD Observer* no. 24 (October 1966): 5; Thorold Masefield, "Co-prosperity and Co-security: Managing the Developed World," *International Affairs* 65, no. 1 (Winter 1988–89): 1; Nicholas Bayne, "Making Sense of Western Economic Policies: The Role of the OECD," *World Today* 43, no. 2 (February 1987): 27–30.

5 OECD, *Getting to Grips with Globalization: The OECD in a Changing World* (Paris: OECD, 2004), 8.

6 Richard Woodward, "The Organization for Economic Cooperation and Development: Meeting the Challenges of the Twenty-First Century?," in *Neo-Liberalism, State Power and Global Governance*, ed. Stephen McBride and Simon Lee (Dordrecht, The Netherlands: Springer, 2007), 232.

7 Quoted in Emile van Lennep, "Japan and the OECD," *OECD Observer* no. 69 (April 1974): 15.

8 Scott Sullivan, *From War to Wealth—Fifty Years of Innovation* (Paris: OECD, 1997), 33.

9 Francis Fukuyama, *The End of History and the Last Man* (London: Penguin, 1992).

10 OECD, *Medium-Term Strategic Objectives C(91) 1* (Paris: OECD, 1991) quoted in Martin Marcussen, "OECD Governance through Soft Law," 122 (emphasis in original).

11 Robert Wolfe, "The Organization for Economic Cooperation and Development," in *Routledge Encyclopedia of International Political Economy*, ed. R. J. Barry Jones (London: Routledge, 2001), 1180.
12 Kerstin Martens and Anja P. Jakobi, "The OECD as Actor in Politics—Introduction," Paper presented to the workshop "Mechanisms of OECD Governance—International Incentives for National Policy Making?" University of Bremen 21–22 September 2007.
13 Per-Olof Busch, "The OECD Environment Directorate: The Art of Persuasion and its Limitations," *GlobGov Global Governance Working Paper No. 20*, October 2006, 3.
14 Ibid., 3.
15 OECD, "Statistics Portal: About," available at www.oecd.org/about/0,3347, en_2825_293564_1_1_1_1_1,00.html (Accessed 2 September 2008); OECD, "Statistical Databases," www.oecd.org/document/44/0,3343,en_21571361_3 3915056_34004076_1_1_1_1,00.html (Accessed 2 September 2008).
16 OECD, "Glossary of Statistical Terms," available at http://stats.oecd.org/glossary/detail.asp?ID=2640 (Accessed 1 September 2008).
17 Quoted in Jean-H. Guilmette, *The Power of Peer Learning: Networks and Development Cooperation* (New Delhi, India: Academic Foundation), 107.
18 OECD, *OECD Environmental Indicators: Development, Measurement and Use*, available at www.oecd.org/dataoecd/7/47/24993546.pdf (Accessed 3 September 2008).
19 Per-Olof Busch, "The OECD Environment Directorate: The Art of Persuasion and its Limitations," 3.
20 Robert Wolfe, "From Reconstructing Europe to Constructing Globalization: The OECD in Historical Perspective," paper presented to the OECD and Global Government Workshop, Carleton University, Canada, 19–20 January 2007.
21 Anonymous, "Top of the Class," *Economist*, 387, no. 8586 (28 June–4 July 2008), 79.
22 James Salzman, "Labor Rights, Globalization and Institutions: the Role and Influence of the Organization for Economic Cooperation and Development," *Michigan Journal of International Law* 21, no. 4 (Summer 2000): 778.
23 Henry G. Aubrey, *Atlantic Economic Cooperation: The Case of the OECD* (New York: Frederick A. Praeger, 1967), 104.
24 James Kanter, "When a Club of Winners Loses Its Way," *International Herald Tribune*, 10 February 2006, available at www.iht.com/articles/2006/02/10/business/wboecd.php?page = 2 (Accessed 1 September 2008).
25 James Salzman, "Labor Rights, Globalization and Institutions: the Role and Influence of the Organization for Economic Cooperation and Development," 778.
26 Marcussen, "OECD Governance through Soft Law," 112.
27 Niels Thygesen, *Peer Pressure as Part of Surveillance by International Institutions* (Paris: OECD, 2002), 2–3.
28 Robert O. Keohane and Joseph S. Nye, "Transgovernmental Relations and International Organizations," *World Politics* 27, no. 1 (October 1974): 45.
29 Aubrey, *Atlantic Economic Cooperation: The Case of the OECD*, 28.
30 Anne-Marie Slaughter, *A New World Order* (Princeton, N.J.: Princeton University Press, 2004), 171–72.
31 Fabrizio Pagani, *Peer Review: A Tool for Cooperation and Change. An Analysis of an OECD Working Method* (Paris: OECD, 2002), 6.

32 OECD Observer, "20 Nations Exchange Their Policy Ideas for Mutual Economic Benefit," *OECD Observer* no. 3 (March 1963): 6.
33 Chris Giles and John Thornhill, "Forum's Chief Calls for Shake-up," *Financial Times*, 26 July 2005, 12.
34 Marcussen, "OECD Governance through Soft Law," 106.
35 OECD, "Convention on the Organisation for Economic Co-operation and Development," available at www.oecd.org/document/7/0,3343,en_2649_344 83_1915847_1_1_1_1,00.html (Accessed 1 September 2008).
36 Nicola Bonucci, "The Legal Status of an OECD Act and the Procedure for Its Adoption," available at www.oecd.org/dataoecd/26/29/31691605.pdf (Accessed 1 September 2008).
37 Ibid.
38 OECD, *Rules of Procedure of the Organization 1992* (Paris: OECD, 1992).
39 Nicola Bonucci, "The Legal Status of an OECD Act and the Procedure for Its Adoption."
40 Ibid.
41 Ibid.
42 Ibid. (my emphasis).
43 Kenneth W. Abbott and Duncan Snidal, "Hard and Soft Law in International Governance," *International Organization* 54, no. 3 (Summer 2000): 421–22.
44 Marcussen, "OECD Governance through Soft Law," 103.
45 OECD, *Convention on Combating Bribery of Foreign Public Officials in International Business Transactions and Related Documents, DAFFE/IME/ BR(97)20* (Paris: OECD, 1997), 8.
46 James Salzman, "Labor Rights, Globalization and Institutions: the Role and Influence of the Organization for Economic Cooperation and Development," 815.
47 Abbott and Snidal, "Hard and Soft Law in International Governance," 445.
48 Joseph S. Nye, *The Paradox of American Power: Why the World's Only Superpower Can't Go It Alone* (Oxford: Oxford University Press, 2002), 144.
49 Busch, "The OECD Environment Directorate: The Art of Persuasion and its Limitations," 7–8.
50 OECD, "The International Network of Pensions Regulators and Supervisors (INPRS) Endorses Principles for Private Occupational Pensions," available at www.oecd.org/document/28/0,3343,en_2649_34853_1918364_119690_1_ 1_1,00.html (Accessed 22 September 2008).
51 Mark Pieth, "Tenth Anniversary of the Anti-bribery convention," available at www.oecd.org/document/62/0,3343,en_21571361_39316778_39525054_1 _1_1,00.html (Accessed 23 September 2008).
52 See Transparency International, *OECD Anti-Bribery Convention Progress Report 2008* (Berlin, Germany: Transparency International, 2008), 10.
53 Ibid., 10.
54 Angel Gurria, "The Tenth Anniversary of the OECD Anti-Bribery Convention: Its Impact and its Achievements," available at www.oecd.org/ document/37/0,3343,en_2649_34487_39656933_1_1_1_1,00.html (Accessed 22 September 2008).
55 OECD, *Convention on Combating Bribery of Foreign Public Officials in International Business Transactions and related Documents*, 6.
56 Martin Marcussen, "The OECD in Search of a Role: Playing the Idea Game," paper presented to European Consortium for Political Research, Grenoble, Switzerland, 6–11 April 2001, 1.

138   *Notes*

57 Henry G. Aubrey, *Atlantic Economic Cooperation: The Case of the OECD*, 7.
58 Nicholas Bayne, "Making Sense of Western Economic Policies: The Role of the OECD," 30.
59 Theodore H. Cohn, *Governing Global Trade: International Institutions in Conflict and Convergence* (Aldershot: Ashgate, 2002), 290.
60 Richard Blackhurst, "The Capacity of the WTO to Fulfill Its Mandate," in *The WTO as an International Organization*, ed. Anne O.Krueger (Chicago, Ill.: University of Chicago Press, 2000), 38–39.
61 WTO, "The WTO and the Organization for Economic Cooperation and Development (OECD)," available at www.wto.org/english/theWTO_e/coher_e/wto_oecd_e.htm (Accessed 20 September 2008).
62 Roy Culpeper, "Systemic Reform at a Standstill: A Flock of "Gs" in Search of Global Financial Stability," available at www.g8.utoronto.ca/scholar/culpeper2000/index.html (Accessed 10 August 2008).
63 Cohn, *Governing Global Trade: International Institutions in Conflict and Convergence*, 63.
64 Bill L. Long, *International Environmental Issues and the OECD 1950–2000* (Paris: OECD, 2000), 74–75.
65 Quoted in Robert Putnam and Nicholas Bayne, *Hanging Together: Cooperation and Conflict in the Seven-Power Summits (2nd edition)* (London: Sage, 1987), 138.
66 Bayne, "Making Sense of Western Economic Policies: The Role of the OECD," 30.
67 Per-Olof Busch, "The OECD Environment Directorate: The Art of Persuasion and its Limitations," 8–9; Bill L. Long, *International Environmental Issues and the OECD 1950–2000*, 83, 88.
68 OECD, "Chair's summary of the OECD Council at Ministerial Level, Paris, 4–5 June 2008—Outreach, Reform and the Economics of Climate Change," available at www.oecd.org/document/56/0,3343,en_2649_201185_40778872_1_1_1_1,00.html (Accessed 1 September 2008).
69 Miriam Camps, *"First World" Relationships: The Role of the OECD* (Paris: The Atlantic Institute for International Affairs, 1975), 46.
70 Salzman, "Labor Rights, Globalization and Institutions: the Role and Influence of the Organization for Economic Cooperation and Development," 797.
71 Ibid.
72 Long, *International Environmental Issues and the OECD 1950–2000*, 128.
73 Scott Sullivan, *From War to Wealth—Fifty Years of Innovation*, 8.
74 Aubrey, *Atlantic Economic Cooperation: The Case of the OECD*, 92, 120.
75 Anonymous, "International Action on the Problems of a Major Growth Industry—Aluminum," *OECD Observer* no. 64 (June 1973): 13.
76 Anonymous, "The Sinking of the MAI," *Economist*, 346, no. 8059 (14–20 March 1998), 105.
77 Camps, *"First World" Relationships: The Role of the OECD*, 39.
78 OECD, "International Futures Programme: About," available online at www.oecd.org/about/0,3347,en_2649_33707_1_1_1_1_1,00.html (Accessed 18 September 2008).
79 Sylvia Ostry, quoted in Anonymous, "International Economic Cooperation Past and Future," *OECD Observer* no. 179 (December 1992-January 1993): S6.
80 Ougaard, *Political Globalization: State, Power and Social Forces*, 86.

4 Current issues

1 OECD, "Chair's Summary of the OECD Council at Ministerial Level, Paris, 15–16 May 2007—Innovation: Advancing the OECD Agenda for Growth and Equity," available at www.oecd.org/document/22/0,2340, en_2649_201185_38604566_1_1_1_1,00.html (Accessed 1 August 2008).
2 OECD, *Annual Report 2006* (Paris: OECD, 2006), 53.
3 OECD, *Agricultural Policies in OECD Countries: At a Glance 2008* (Paris: OECD, 2008), 4.
4 OECD, *Development Cooperation Report 2007* (Paris: OECD, 2008), 134.
5 OECD, "Partnerships in Statistics for Development in the 21st Century (PARIS21) Web Site," available at www.oecd.org/document/9/0,3343, en_2649_34585_1896905_1_1_1_1,00.html (Accessed 29 July 2008).
6 OECD, *OECD Development Assistance Committee. … where governments come together to make aid work* (Paris: OECD, 2007), 38–39.
7 OECD, "About the OECD Global Forum on Development," available at www.oecd.org/document/59/0,3343,en_21571361_37824719_37824763_1_1_1_1,00.html (Accessed 28 July 2008).
8 See OECD, *Active in Africa* (Paris: OECD, 2008).
9 OECD, *Development Cooperation Report 2007*, 137.
10 See Sven Steinmo, "The Evolution of Policy Ideas: Tax Policy in the 20th Century," *The British Journal of Politics and International Relations* 5, no. 2 (May 2003): 206–36; John Hobson, "Disappearing Taxes or the "Race to the Middle"? Fiscal Policy in the OECD," in *States in the Global Economy: Bringing Domestic Institutions Back In*, ed. Linda Weiss (Cambridge: Cambridge University Press, 2003), 37–57.
11 On the origins of the Model Tax Convention see OECD, *Model Tax Convention on Income and on Capital (Updated as of 29 April 2000): Volume 1* (Paris: OECD, 2000), 1–6.
12 OECD, *The OECD's Project on Harmful Tax Practices: 2006 Update on Progress in Member Countries* (Paris: OECD, 2006), 3–6.
13 OECD, "Tax Information Exchange Agreements," available at www.oecd.org/document/7/0,3343,en_2649_33745_38312839_1_1_1_1,00.html (Accessed 24 July 2008).
14 OECD, "Competition Law and Policy: About," available at www.oecd.org/about/0,3347,en_2649_34685_1_1_1_1_1,00.html (Accessed 15 July 2008).
15 See Brendan Sweeney, "Export Cartels: Is There a Need for Global Rules?," *Journal of International Economic Law* 10, no. 1 (February 2007): 87–115; Katalin J. Cseres, Maarten P. Schinkel, and Floris O. W. Vogelaar, eds, *Criminalization of Competition Law Enforcement: Economic and Legal Implications for the EU Member States* (Cheltenham: Edward Elgar, 2006).
16 OECD, "International Gateway for Financial Education: About," available at www.oecd.org/pages/0,3417,en_39665975_39667032_1_1_1_1_1,00.html (Accessed 1 August 2008).
17 OECD, *Forty Years' Experience with the OECD Code of Liberalization of Capital Movements* (Paris: OECD, 2002).
18 See Bill L. Long, *International Environmental Issues and the OECD 1950–2000* (Paris: OECD, 2000).
19 OECD, *OECD Annual Report 2007* (Paris: OECD, 2007), 40.
20 OECD, *OECD Work on Environment 2007–2008* (Paris: OECD, 2007), 4.

21 OECD, *OECD Environmental Strategy for the First Decade of the 21st Century* (Paris: OECD, 2001).

22 See OECD, *The Distributional Effects of Environmental Policy* (Paris: OECD, 2006).

23 OECD, *OECD Environmental Outlook to 2030* (Paris: OECD, 2008).

24 OECD, *OECD Key Environmental Indicators 2008* (Paris: OECD, 2008).

25 See OECD, "Chair's Summary of the OECD Council at Ministerial Level, Paris, 4–5 June 2008—Outreach, Reform and the Economics of Climate Change," available at www.oecd.org/document/56/0,3343,en_2649_201185_40778872_1_1_1_1,00.html (Accessed 16 July 2008).

26 Long, *International Environmental Issues and the OECD 1950–2000*, 124.

27 OECD, *Guidelines for Testing of Chemicals: Full List of Test Guidelines August 2007* available at www.oecd.org/dataoecd/9/11/33663321.pdf (Accessed 15 July 2008).

28 OECD, *OECD Work on Environment 2007–2008*, 12.

29 Thomas Homer-Dixon, "The Rise of Complex Terrorism," *Foreign Policy* no. 128 (January-February 2002): 52–62.

30 OECD, "Steel: About," available at www.oecd.org/about/0,3347,en_2649_34221_1_1_1_1,00.html (Accessed 21 July 2008); OECD, *Annual Report 2005* (Paris: OECD, 2005), 33.

31 IEA, "About the IEA," available at www.iea.org/about/index.asp (Accessed 29 July 2008).

32 Group of Eight, "Gleneagles Plan of Action: Climate Change, Clean Energy and Sustainable Development," available at www.g8.utoronto.ca/summit/2005gleneagles/climatechangeplan.html (Accessed 29 July 2008).

33 IEA, *Towards a Sustainable Energy Future: IEA Programme of Work on Climate Change, Clean Energy and Sustainable Development* (Paris: OECD/IEA, 2008).

34 Group of Eight, "Hokkaido Official Documents: Environment and Climate Change," available at www.g8.utoronto.ca/summit/2008hokkaido/2008-climate.html (Accessed 29 July 2008).

35 NEA, *NEA Annual Report 2007* (Paris: OECD/NEA, 2007), 2, 42.

36 Henry G. Aubrey, *Atlantic Economic Cooperation: The Case of the OECD* (New York: Frederick A. Praeger, 1967), 72–73.

37 Stephen McBride, Kathleen McNutt, and Russell A. Williams, "Policy Learning? The OECD and Its Jobs Strategy," in *The OECD and Transnational Governance*, ed. Rianne Mahon and Stephen McBride (Vancouver, Canada: UBC Press, 2008), 152–69.

38 OECD, *Annual Report '2007*, 12.

39 OECD, "The OECD 'Sickness, Disability and Work' Project," available at www.oecd.org/document/20/0,3343,en_2649_34747_38887124_1_1_1_1,00.html (Accessed 23 July 2008).

40 OECD, "OECD Launches Jobs for Youth project," available at www.oecd.org/document/59/0,3343,en_2649_34747_38019131_1_1_1_1,00.html (Accessed 23 July 2008).

41 OECD, *Live Longer, Work Longer* (Paris: OECD, 2006).

42 OECD, "Towards a Sustainable Future: Communiqué, Paris, 17 May 2001," available at www.g7.utoronto.ca/oecd/oecd2001.htm (Accessed 23 July 2008).

43 OECD, *Jobs for Immigrants (Vol. 1): Labour Market Integration in Australia, Denmark, Germany and Sweden* (Paris: OECD, 2007).

44 Risto Rinne, Johanna Kallo, and Sanna Hokka, "Too Eager to Comply? OECD Education Policies and the Finnish Response," *European Educational Research Journal* 3, no. 2 (2004): 456.
45 On the early years of education at the OECD see George S. Papadopoulos, *Education 1960–90: The OECD Perspective* (Paris: OECD, 1994).
46 OECD, *Lifelong Learning For All: Meeting of the Education Committee at Ministerial Level, 16–17 January 1996* (Paris: OECD, 1996).
47 Kjell Rubenson, "OECD Education Policies and World Hegemony," in *The OECD and Transnational Governance*, ed. Rianne Mahon and Stephen McBride (Vancouver, Canada: UBC Press, 2008), 242–59.
48 OECD, *OECD Work on Education* (Paris: OECD, 2006), 5.
49 Anonymous, "Top of the Class," *Economist*, 387, no. 8586 (28 June–4 July 2008), 79.
50 OECD, "OECD Programme for International Student Assessment (PISA): Participating Countries," available at www.oecd.org/pages/0,3417,en_32252 351_32236225_1_1_1_1_1,00.html (Accessed 1 September 2008).
51 Roser Cusso, "Restructuring UNESCO's Statistical Services—The 'sad story' of UNESCO's Education Statistics: 4 Years Later," *International Journal of Educational Development* 26, no. 5 (September 2006): 533.
52 OECD, *Starting Strong II: Early Childhood Education and Care* (Paris: OECD, 2006).
53 See for example Australian Labor Party, "Federal Labor Releases Blueprint for Reform of Early Childhood Services," 16 November 2007, available at http://mobile.alp.org.au/media/1107/msedutfcshealoo161.php (Accessed 4 August 2008).
54 See OECD, "Health Care Quality Indicators Project," available at www.oecd.org/document/34/0,3343,en_2649_33929_37088930_1_1_1_37407,00.html (Accessed 17 July 2008).
55 OECD, "Health Data: About," available at www.oecd.org/about/0,3347,en_2649_34631_1_1_1_1_1,00.html (Accessed 7 July 2008).
56 See Bob Deacon and Alexandra Kaasch, "The OECD's Social and Health Policy: Neo-liberal Stalking Horse or Balancer of Social and Economic Objectives?" in *The OECD and Transnational Governance*, ed. Rianne Mahon and Stephen McBride (Vancouver, Canada: UBC Press, 2008), 226–41.
57 OECD, "OECD Health Data 2008—Frequently Requested Data," available at www.oecd.org/document/16/0,3343,en_2649_34631_2085200_1_1_1_1,00.html (Accessed 14 July 2008).

5 OECD reform

1 Jorma Julin, "The OECD: Securing the Future," *OECD Observer* no. 240–41 (December 2003): 41.
2 OECD, *A Strategy for Enlargement and Outreach: Report by the Chair of the Heads of Delegation Working Group on the Enlargement Strategy and Outreach, Ambassador Seiichiro Noburu* (Paris: OECD, 2004), 16.
3 Angel Gurria, "Ensuring a Smoother Flight," *OECD Observer* no. 264–65 (December 2007–January 2008): 3.
4 Quoted in James Kanter, "When a Club of Winners Loses Its Way," *International Herald Tribune*, 10 February 2006, available at www.iht.com/articles/2006/02/10/business/wboecd.php (Accessed 30 August 2008).

5 OECD, "OECD Council Resolution on Enlargement and Enhanced Engagement," available at www.oecd.org/document/7/0,3343,en_2649_2011 85_38604487_1_1_1_1,00.html (Accessed 31 August 2008).
6 The road maps are available at www.olis.oecd.org/olis/2007doc.nsf/ ENGDIRCORPLOOK?OpenView&Start=1&Count=100&Expand=5.2.2# 5.2.2 (Accessed 31 August 2008).
7 OECD, *Meeting of the Council at Ministerial Level, 4–5 June 2008: Report to Ministers on Accession* (Paris: OECD, 2008), 3.
8 World Bank, "Gross Domestic Product 2007, PPP," available at http://sitere sources.worldbank.org/DATASTATISTICS/Resources/GDP_PPP.pdf (Accessed 1 September 2008).
9 Ibid.
10 OECD, *A Strategy for Enlargement and Outreach*, 7.
11 Advisory Council on International Affairs, *The OECD of the Future* (The Hague, The Netherlands: Advisory Council on International Affairs, 2007), 10.
12 OECD, "OECD Council Resolution on Enlargement and Enhanced Engagement."
13 OECD, *A Strategy for Enlargement and Outreach*, 21, 49.
14 Confidential interview with a senior OECD official, 18 June 2008.
15 Anonymous, "A Bowl of Thin Alphabet Soup," *Economist*, 388 no. 8596 (9–15 August 2008), 58.
16 OECD, *Getting to Grips with Globalization: The OECD in a Changing World* (Paris: OECD, 2004), 29; OECD, *The OECD's Global Relations Programme 2007–08* (Paris: OECD, 2007), 9.
17 Paul Betts, "Navigating the OECD 'Supertanker'," *Financial Times*, 3 March 2003, 13.
18 Christopher Adams, "Think-tank Rethinks Its Role," *Financial Times*, 24 September 1999, 4.
19 OECD, *A Strategy for Enlargement and Outreach*, 49–50.
20 OECD, "Chair's Summary of the OECD Council at Ministerial Level, Paris, 4–5 June 2008—Outreach, Reform and the Economics of Climate Change," available at www.oecd.org/document/56/0,3343,en_2649_34487_4 0778872_1_1_1_1,00.html (Accessed 31 August 2008).
21 Advisory Council on International Affairs, *The OECD of the Future*, 13.
22 These issues are explored by various contributors to Andrew F. Cooper and Agata Antkiewicz, ed., *Emerging Powers in Global Governance: Lessons from the Heiligendamm Process* (Waterloo, Canada: Wilfrid Laurier Press, 2008).
23 Anonymous, "RI needs more Liberalization: OECD," *Jakarta Post*, 25 July 2008, available at www.thejakartapost.com/news/2008/07/25/ri-needs-more-liberalization-oecd.html (Accessed 31 August 2008).
24 OECD, *A General Procedure for Future Accessions C(2007)31/FINAL* (Paris: OECD, 2007), 4.
25 OECD, *The OECD's Global Relations Programme 2007–08*, 14.
26 This section draws upon Richard Woodward, "Towards Complex Multilateralism? Civil Society and the OECD," in *The OECD and Transnational Governance*, ed. Rianne Mahon and Stephen McBride (Vancouver, Canada: UBC Press, 2008), 77–95.
27 Helmut Anheier, Marlies Glasius, and Mary Kaldor, "Concepts of Global Civil Society," in *Global Civil Society 2001*, ed. Helmut Anheier, Marlies Glasius, and Mary Kaldor (Oxford: Oxford University Press, 2001), 12–15.

28 Jan Aart Scholte, "Civil Society and Governance in the Global Policy," in *Towards a Global Polity*, ed. Morten Ougaard and Richard A. Higgott (London: Routledge, 2002), 146.

29 See for example Richard Falk, *Predatory Globalization: A Critique* (Cambridge: Polity, 1999).

30 Robert O'Brien, Anne Marie Goetz, Jan Aart Scholte, and Marc Williams, *Contesting Global Governance: Multilateral Economic Institutions and Global Social Movements* (Cambridge: Cambridge University Press, 2000), 3.

31 Ibid.

32 OECD, *Decision of the Council on Relations with International Non-Governmental Organizations OECD Doc C(62)45 (1962)* (Paris: OECD, 1962).

33 John West, "Emergence of Multi-stakeholder Diplomacy at the OECD: Origins, Lessons and Directions for the Future," Paper presented to the International Conference on Multi-Stakeholder Diplomacy, Malta, 11–13 February 2005, 7–11.

34 OECD, *Annual Report 2007* (Paris: OECD, 2007), 85.

35 OECD, *Annual Report 2006* (Paris: OECD, 2006), 86.

36 OECD, "Welcome to SourceOECD," available at http://titania.sourceoecd. org/vl=8575723/cl=24/nw=1/rpsv/home.htm (Accessed 29 August 2008).

37 OECD, *OECD's Cooperative Work with Civil Society C/INF(2006)24* (Paris: OECD, 2006).

38 James Salzman, "Decentralized Administrative Law in the Organization for Economic Cooperation and Development," *Law and Contemporary Problems* 68, no. 3-4 (Summer-Autumn 2005): 217.

39 OECD Watch, "Members," available at www.oecdwatch.org/413.htm (Accessed 29 August 2008).

40 OECD Watch, "Background," available at www.oecdwatch.org/419.htm (Accessed 29 August 2008).

41 OECD, *Policy Brief: Civil Society and the OECD* (Paris: OECD, 2005), 5.

42 James Salzman, "Decentralized Administrative Law in the Organization for Economic Cooperation and Development," 200–203.

43 OECD, *Policy Brief: Civil Society and the OECD*, 3.

44 OECD, *Fighting Corruption: What Role for Civil Society? The Experience of the OECD* (Paris: OECD, 2003), 11–18.

45 West, "Emergence of Multi-stakeholder Diplomacy at the OECD: Origins, Lessons and Directions for the Future," 10–11.

46 Monica Blagescu and Robert Lloyd, *2006 Global Accountability Report: Holding Power to Account* (London: One World Trust, 2006), 37.

47 OECD, "Who Came to OECD Annual Forum 2002?" quoted in Richard Woodward, "The Organization for Economic Cooperation and Development," *New Political Economy* 9, no. 1 (March 2004): 120.

48 Robert W. Cox, "Civil Society at the Turn of the Millennium: Prospects For an Alternative World Order," *Review of International Studies* 25, no. 3 (January 1999): 12.

49 Morten Ougaard, "The OECD's Global Role," Paper presented at the workshop "Mechanisms of OECD Governance—International Incentives for National Policy Making?" University of Bremen, 21–22 September 2007.

50 See for example, Helmut K. Anheier, Mary Kaldor, and Marlies Glasius, eds, *Global Civil Society 2006/7* (London: Sage, 2007).

144   *Notes*

51 TUAC, *Governing the Global Economy: What Role for the OECD?* (Paris: TUAC, 2005), 3.
52 Michael C. Webb, "Defining the Boundaries of Legitimate State Practice: Norms, Transnational Actors and the OECD's Project on Harmful Tax Competition," *Review of International Political Economy* 11, no. 4 (October 2004): 812.
53 OECD Watch, *Five Years On: A Review of the OECD Guidelines and National Contact Points*, available at www.oecdwatch.org/docs/OECD_Watch_5_years_on.pdf (Accessed 30 August 2008), 15.
54 Patricia Feeney of OECD Watch, quoted in Hugh Williamson, "NGOs Voice Doubts on Next OECD Chief," *Financial Times*, 30 November 2005, 4.
55 Robert O'Brien, Anne Marie Goetz, Jan Aart Scholte, and Marc Williams, *Contesting Global Governance: Multilateral Economic Institutions and Global Social Movements*, 215–16.
56 James Kanter, "A Major Face-lift for OECD?," *International Herald Tribune*, 29 November 2005, available at www.iht.com/articles/2005/11/29/business/oecd.php?page = 2 (Accessed 30 August 2008).
57 Hugh Williamson, "NGOs Voice Doubts on Next OECD Chief," 4.
58 OECD, "Receiving Globalist of the Year Award, Angel Gurria Stresses the Importance of Multilateral Cooperation," available at www.oecd.org/document/53/0,3343,en_2649_201185_39544181_1_1_1_1,00.html (Accessed 21 August 2008).
59 OECD Watch, *Newsletter April 2008*, available at www.oecdwatch.org/docs/OECD_Watch_Newsletter_April_2008_English.pdf (Accessed 30 August 2008), 2.
60 See for example Hugo Dobson, *The Group of 7/8* (London: Routledge, 2007).
61 Nicholas Bayne, *Hanging in There: The G7 and G8 Summit in Maturity and Renewal* (Aldershot: Ashgate, 2000), 90.
62 G. John Ikenberry, "Salvaging the G-7," *Foreign Affairs* 72, no. 2 (Spring 1993): 136–38; Andrea de Guttry, "The Institutional Configuration of the G-7 in the New International Scenario," *The International Spectator* 29, no. 2 (April-June 1994), 76.
63 Donald Johnston, "Look no Further for a Home for Global Bodies," *Financial Times*, 28 November 2005, 13.
64 OECD, *The OECD at Work* (Paris: OECD, 1964), 6.
65 Bayne, *Hanging in There: The G7 and G8 Summit in Maturity and Renewal*, 62.
66 Ibid., 8.
67 Donald Johnston, "Look no Further for a Home for Global Bodies," 13.
68 Group of Eight, "Growth and Responsibility in the World Economy: Summit Declaration, Heiligendamm, June 7, 2007," available at www.g8.utoronto.ca/summit/2007heiligendamm/g8-2007-economy.html (Accessed 26 August 2008).
69 Group of Eight, "Joint Statement by the German G8 Presidency and the Heads of State and/or Government of Brazil, China, India, Mexico and South Africa on the Occasion of the G8 Summit in Heiligendamm," available at www.g8.utoronto.ca/summit/2007heiligendamm/g8-2007-joint.html (Accessed 26 August 2008).
70 Thomas Fues and Julia Leininger, "Germany and the Heiligendamm Process," in *Emerging Powers in Global Governance: Lessons from the*

Heiligendamm Process, ed. Andrew F. Cooper and Agata Antkiewicz (Waterloo, Canada: Wilfred Laurier Press, 2008), 248–49.

71 Steering Committee of the Heiligendamm Process, *Interim Report on the Heiligendamm Process at the G8 Summit in Hokkaido Toyako 7 to 9 July 2008*, available at www.g8summit.go.jp/doc/pdf/0709_01_en.pdf (Accessed 27 August 2008).

72 Anonymous, "They Came, They Jawed, They Failed to Conquer," *Economist*, 388, no. 8588 (12–18 July 2008), 76.

73 Matei Hoffman, "Building Global Partnerships," *OECD Observer* no. 261 (May 2007): 5.

74 Bayne, *Hanging in There: The G7 and G8 Summit in Maturity and Renewal*, 3, 14.

75 de Guttry, "The Institutional Configuration of the G-7 in the New International Scenario," 74.

76 John J. Kirton, "Explaining G8 Effectiveness," in *The G8's Role in the New Millennium*, ed. Michael R. Hodges, John J. Kirton, and Joseph P. Daniels (Aldershot: Ashgate, 1999), 45.

77 Ikenberry, "Salvaging the G-7," 132.

78 See for example Gill Hubbard and David Miller, ed., *Arguments Against G8* (London: Pluto Press, 2005).

79 Julin, "The OECD: Securing the Future."

80 James Salzman, "Decentralized Administrative Law in the Organization for Economic Cooperation and Development," 195.

6 The future of the OECD

1 David Held, Anthony McGrew, David Goldblatt, and Jonathan Perraton, *Global Transformations: Politics, Economics and Culture* (Cambridge: Polity, 1999), 3–4.

2 Ibid., 5–14.

3 Anonymous, "What a Way to Run the World," *Economist*, 387, no. 8587 (5–11 July 2008), 16.

4 Anonymous, "Wrestling for Influence," *Economist*, 387, no. 8587 (5–11 July 2008), 39.

5 David Henderson, "The Role of the OECD in Liberalising International Trade and Capital Flows," *The World Economy* 19, no. 5 (September 1996): 23.

6 Henry G. Aubrey, *Atlantic Economic Cooperation: The Case of the OECD* (New York: Frederick A. Praeger, 1967), 109.

7 Richard Woodward, "The Organisation for Economic Cooperation and Development," *New Political Economy* 9, no. 1 (March 2004): 121.

8 See for example Anonymous, "Wrestling for Influence," 37–40; Miles Kahler, "Defining Accountability Up: The Global Economic Multilaterals," *Government and Opposition* 39, no. 2 (Spring 2004): 132–58.

9 Anne-Marie Slaughter, "Government Networks, World Order, and the G20," Paper presented at the IDRC, Ottawa, 29 February 2004, 17.

10 Jorma Julin, "The OECD: Securing the Future," *OECD Observer* no. 240–41 (December 2003): 50.

11 Joseph S. Nye, *Soft Power: The Means to Success in World Politics* (New York: Public Affairs, 2004).

12 Anne-Marie Slaughter, "The Real New World Order," *Foreign Affairs* 76, no. 5 (September–October 1997): 196.

13 OECD, *Annual Report 2008* (Paris: OECD, 2008), 7.
14 Anonymous, "Trouble at the OECD," *Economist*, 383, no. 8525 (21–27 April 2007), 16; OECD, "Statement by the Secretary-General, Angel Gurria, in Reply to An Article in The Economist of 20 April 2007," available at www.oecd.org/document/38/0,3343,en_2649_201185_38438438_1_1_1_1,00.html (Accessed 5 August 2008).

Select bibliography and electronic resources

General works on the OECD: organizational features, history, evolution

The OECD has published several books advertising its own work. While yielding interesting insights into the nature, structure and culture of the organization, they offer little critical analysis.

OECD, *O.E.C.D.: History, Aims, Structure* (Paris: OECD, 1971).

OEEC, *A Decade of Co-operation Achievements and Perspectives*: *9th Report of the OEEC* (Paris: OEEC, 1958).

Scott Sullivan, *From War to Wealth: Fifty Years of Innovation* (Paris: OECD, 1997).

More critical literature written by academic commentators and OEEC/OECD practitioners includes:

Henry G. Aubrey, *Atlantic Economic Cooperation: The Case of the OECD* (New York: Frederick A. Praeger, 1967).

Nicholas Bayne, "Making Sense of Western Economic Policies: The Role of the OECD," *World Today* 43, no. 2 (February 1987): 27–30. The UK's Permanent Representative to the OECD from 1985–88 explores the OECD's role and offers insights into the breadth of its operations.

Miriam Camps, *"First World" Relationships: The Role of the OECD* (Paris: The Atlantic Institute for International Affairs, 1975); Lincoln Gordon, "The Organization for European Economic Cooperation," *International Organization* 10, no. 1 (February 1956): 1–11. Two former U.S. State Department employees who were intimately involved with the Marshall Plan reflect on the emergence and evolution of the OEEC/OECD and their role in sponsoring and managing Western interdependence.

David Henderson, "The Role of the OECD in Liberalising International Trade and Capital Flows," *The World Economy* 19, no. 1 (January 1996): 11–27.

The former head of the OECD Economics and Statistics Department probes the organization's role in the liberalization of trade and finance.

Martin Marcussen, "OECD Governance through Soft Law," in *Soft Law in Governance and Regulation: An Interdisciplinary Analysis*, ed. Ulrika Morth (Cheltenham, U.K.: Edward Elgar, 2004), 103–26. An excellent overview of the OECD's "soft law" capabilities.

Robert Wolfe, *The Making of the Peace, 1993: The OECD in Canadian Economic Diplomacy* (Kingston, Canada: Queen's University Centre for International Relations, 1993). Wolfe supplies an overview of the OECD's historical development, its role in the Cold War economic and security environment, and uses the OECD as a laboratory for studying international cooperation. Wolfe was a member of the Canadian Delegation to the OECD from 1981 to 1985.

Richard Woodward, "Global Monitor: The Organization for Economic Cooperation and Development," *New Political Economy* 9, no. 1 (March 2004): 113–27. Audits recent developments at the OECD including the likely impact of the proposed enlargement and outreach program.

OECD work on contemporary issues

The *OECD Annual Report* and the *Key Information* booklet produced to support the Ministerial Council Meeting précis recent OECD activity. These are available from the OECD website (see below).

Klaus Armingeon and Michelle Beyeler, eds, *The OECD and European Welfare States* (Cheltenham, U.K.: Edward Elgar, 2004). Provides an overview of the OECD's analyses and recommendations on social issues and their impact on welfare states in Western Europe.

David J. Blair, *Trade Negotiations in the OECD: Structures, Institutions and States* (London: Kegan Paul International, 1993); Theodore H. Cohn, *Governing Global Trade: International institutions in conflict and convergence* (Aldershot, U.K.: Ashgate, 2002). These two titles provide comprehensive accounts of the OECD's role in the global trading regime.

Rianne Mahon and Stephen McBride, eds, *The OECD and Transnational Governance* (Vancouver, Canada: UBC Press, 2008). This book examines the nature of the OECD as an international institution and elaborates current OECD work in the fields of labor, health, education, competition policy, genetic licensing, foreign investment, public management, and social policy.

OECD, *Development Assistance Committee in Dates: Prepared for the 40th Anniversary of the Development Assistance Group/Development Assistance Committee* (Paris: OECD, 2000). Overview of the membership, mandate, and main accomplishments of the DAC.

Michael C. Webb, "Defining the Boundaries of Legitimate State Practice: Norms, Transnational Actors and the OECD's Project on Harmful Tax Competition," *Review of International Political Economy* 11, no. 4 (October

2004): 787–827. Details the OECD's ill-fated harmful tax competition initiative.

The future of the OECD

Jorma Julin, "The OECD: Securing the Future," *OECD Observer* no. 240–41 (December 2003): 48–50. The Finnish ambassador to the OECD from 2000–05 argues that reform is essential for the OECD to retain its relevance.

OECD, *The OECD: Challenges and Strategic Objectives: 1997: Note by the Secretary General, C(97)180* (Paris: OECD, 1997). Donald Johnston spells out his vision for the future of the OECD.

———— *A Strategy for Enlargement and Outreach: Report by the Chair of the Heads of Delegation Working Group on the Enlargement Strategy and Outreach, Ambassador Seiichiro Noburu* (Paris: OECD, 2004). The final report of the Working Group on Enlargement and Outreach containing its main recommendations to the OECD Council.

———— *Getting to Grips with Globalization: The OECD in a Changing World* (Paris: OECD, 2004). An appraisal of the OECD's recent activities and future challenges. Useful appendices containing information about the secretariat, the budget and recent reforms.

Richard Woodward, "Age Concern: The Future of the OECD," *World Today* 62, no. 8–9 (August–September 2006): 38–39. Concise overview of the problems confronting the OECD and its proposed reform strategy.

Electronic resources

www.oecd.org—The OECD's main website, available in English and French.

www.oecdobserver.org—In-house magazine providing commentary on contemporary issues of relevance to the organization and its members.

www.sourceoecd.org—The OECD's online library of books, statistical databases and periodicals.

www.oecdwatch.org—OECD Watch is a coalition of civil society organizations monitoring the work of the OECD's Investment Committee and the efficacy of the OECD Guidelines for Multinational Enterprises.

Index

Amano, Mari 50
Andorra 89
Argentina 33, 55
Askey, Thelma 50, 105
Australia 2, 45, 47, 66, 100; accession to OECD 23; OECD reform and 108
Austria 2, 14, 45, 47, 53, 63
authoritarian regimes 7; disintegration of 32; OECD members as 6, 108

Bank for International Settlements (BIS) 20; membership of OECD bodies 54, 60; role in European Payments Union 15;
Bayne, Nicholas 75
Belgium 2, 14, 17, 45, 47, 53
Benterbusch, Ulrich 120
Bolivia 55
Brazil 33; enhanced engagement program 42, 105–6, 109; Heiligendamm Process 119; membership of OECD bodies 55; participation in OECD 36, 55, 59, 83, 85; prospective OECD membership 103, 106, 108
Bretton Woods: collapse of 12, 24; changing role of OECD and 20, 28; institutions 126
Brown, Gordon 70
Bulgaria 55, 85, 106
Busch, Per-Olof 65
Bush, George W. Snr. 12
Business and Industry Advisory Committee (BIAC): 46, 110; membership of 55; participation in OECD work 36, 46, 55–6, 112, 115, 116.

Canada 2, 18, 21, 34, 47, 101; associate member of OEEC 15; budget contribution 45; member of WP3 20
Centre for Co-operation with non-Members (CCNM) 35
Centre for Tax Policy and Administration (CTPA) 35, 54, 87
Chemicals Committee 53
Chernobyl 96
Chile: accession negotiations 42, 105–6; participation in OECD bodies 55, 59, 101–2
China 33, 64, 80; enhanced engagement 42, 105–6, 109; Heiligendamm Process 119; participation in OECD 36, 55, 59, 83, 84–5; prospective OECD membership 103, 106, 108
Chinese Taipei 55
civil society Civil Society Coordinators Network 37; defined 109; enlargement and outreach programme and 36–7, 109–17, 122, 127; MAI collapse and 37–8; participation in OECD 7, 40, 44, 53, 54–6, 58, 86
cognitive governance 6–7, 62, 63–4; OECD reform and 104, 105
Cold War: cognitive governance and 6–7, 63–4, 80; effects on OECD xii, xiii, 12, 17, 32–3; G8 role since 117
Committee for Agriculture 112
Centre for Educational Research and Innovation (CERI) 99

Three Mile Island 96
Trade Committee 22, 26, 37, 117
Trade Union Advisory Committee
    (TUAC): 116; membership of 55;
    participation in OECD work 36, 46,
    55–6, 112–13, 116.
Transparency International 74, 113, 116
Truman, Harry 13
Turkey 2, 3, 6, 14, 47, 108; budget
    contribution 45

Uganda 55, 105
Ukraine 55, 85
United Kingdom 2, 14, 28, 46, 47, 101;
    budget contribution 45;
    lack of ministerial presence 48;
    OEEC and 17, 18; WP3
    membership 20
United Nations 23
United Nations Development
    Programme (UNDP) 3
United Nations Environment
    Programme (UNEP) 73, 76, 92
United Nations Educational,
    Scientific and Cultural
    Organization (UNESCO) 86,
    99, 100
United Nations Framework
    Convention on Climate Change
    (UNFCCC) 92

United States 2, 46, 47; budget
    contribution 45; hegemonic
    influence on OEEC 12–15; lack of
    support for John-Claude Paye 34;
    role in harmful tax competition
    initiative 34; transition to OECD
    and 15–18; Versailles Summit and 77
Uruguay 55
US-Canada Free Trade Agreement 34
USSR (see Soviet Union)

Vietnam War 25

Warsaw Pact 17
Wolfe, Robert 65
Working Party Number 3 on Policies
    for the Promotion of Better
    International Payments Equilibrium
    (WP3): effectiveness 20–1, 23;
    membership 20; sidelined in Plaza
    and Louvre Accords 29
World Economic Forum 104
World Health Organization (WHO)
    40, 54
World Trade Organization (WTO):
    Doha Round 84; OECD support
    for 75–6, 84–5; participation in
    OECD work 54, 60

Yemen 105